Protected
by
Angels

Protected by Angels

Magical True Stories of Angelic Intervention

JACKY NEWCOMB

HAY HOUSE

Australia • Canada • Hong Kong • India
South Africa • United Kingdom • United States

First published and distributed in the United Kingdom by:
Hay House UK Ltd, 292B Kensal Rd, London W10 5BE.
Tel.: (44) 20 8962 1230; Fax: (44) 20 8962 1239.
www.hayhouse.co.uk

Published and distributed in the United States of America by:
Hay House, Inc., PO Box 5100, Carlsbad, CA 92018-5100.
Tel.: (1) 760 431 7695 or (800) 654 5126; Fax: (1) 760 431 6948 or (800) 650 5115.
www.hayhouse.com

Published and distributed in Australia by:
Hay House Australia Ltd, 18/36 Ralph St, Alexandria NSW 2015.
Tel.: (61) 2 9669 4299; Fax: (61) 2 9669 4144.
www.hayhouse.com.au

Published and distributed in the Republic of South Africa by:
Hay House SA (Pty), Ltd, PO Box 990, Witkoppen 2068.
Tel./Fax: (27) 11 467 8904. www.hayhouse.co.za

Published and distributed in India by:
Hay House Publishers India, Muskaan Complex, Plot No.3, B-2,
Vasant Kunj, New Delhi – 110 070. Tel.: (91) 11 4176 1620; Fax: (91) 11 4176 1630.
www.hayhouse.co.in

Distributed in Canada by:
Raincoast, 9050 Shaughnessy St, Vancouver, BC V6P 6E5.
Tel.: (1) 604 323 7100; Fax: (1) 604 323 2600

Text © Jacky Newcomb, 2012

The moral rights of the author have been asserted.

A catalogue record for this book is available from the British Library.

ISBN: 978-1-84850-778-4

Printed and bound in Great Britain by TJ International, Padstow, Cornwall.

'…the fountain of all angel knowledge…'
Tony Stockwell

Special love to Peyton x

*To my wonderful fans – thank you for your
continued support and love. May your life
bring you everything that you wish for yourself!
Lots of love
Jacky x*

Contents

Introduction

DEAR READER...

The sun is shining down on the clear blue waters below, leaving a breath-taking glimmer, like diamonds on the waves. It's not for the first time that I give a silent word of thanks to my angels for anchoring me here in Cornwall, England, at this challenging time on Earth. Many times my husband John and I park our car in the car park above the cliffs so we can watch the bedazzling sunsets: the sunlight splitting into orange, reds, pinks and purples, layering the sky like some exotic *mille-feuille,* and finally coming to rest on the horizon before silently putting herself to bed.

As I write this I am sitting on a rock overlooking the sea at Tintagel. Tintagel is on the north coast of Cornwall, and is associated with the mystical legend of King Arthur and his Knights of the Round Table. King Arthur's castle itself can be reached by walking down the many steps from the top of the cliff; erosion over the years has meant that a bridge had to be built for locals and tourists to reach this magical place.

Cornwall is one of the most magical places on Earth and I'm lucky enough to call it my home. The energy of this breathtaking location makes it easy for me to connect with my angels and guides. The blissful feeling I carry with me most of the time must surely be partly associated with this place of magic. Yet angels are everywhere: in the darkest of locations and the lightest of vibrations. They follow us to work and sit with us while we study; they're with us wherever we roam, though they draw especially close when we request their help. Angels long to assist us as we go about our daily lives. Their roles are to help and protect us.

In this exciting new book we shall explore together the angels' roles and purposes; of course I shall illustrate everything with wonderful real-life stories, as I always do. Your very own magical encounters with these beings of light are sent to me from all over the world.

Angels are real beings, not tales of make-believe. Normal everyday people have experienced moments of comfort from unseen hands holding theirs; a reassuring hug or hand on the shoulder from something invisible... and sometimes even a supportive voice from the darkness that whispers that everything is going to be OK.

EARTH CHANGES

Angels have always watched over their human charges, but gather close during times of change. Previously they have assembled in groups as countries have gone to war or during times of earthly tragedies like tornados and earthquakes.

Our Earth is now going through a different type of transition. The energy of our planet is speeding up to a higher vibration; many of you can already feel this change happening in your own life. Our lives will be forever changed… but in a good way.

BODY CHANGES

Lots of us have found we can no longer eat foods that we've always been able to. Sugar, processed foods and household chemicals are causing problems in our lives. Allergies appear where they never have before. Our bodies are craving raw, natural, organic and pure foods and products. The less merchandise has been messed around with, the better – the more local a product is, the less distance it has to travel and the better for the environment. Shorter distances mean fewer lorries on the road, less fuel used and fresher produce. The country roads around my home are full of allotments, sectioned areas of land where people have moved right back to 'growing their own'.

Many of us are already noticing changes in our psychic abilities. How many times do you find yourself saying, 'Oh, I was just thinking that too!' or 'I knew you were going to say that!' More and more of our communication will be non-verbal. It's as if our telepathic skills have been re-awakened. Most other races around the universe don't rely on verbal communication at all. Ideas will be communicated to you from your guides and angels in blocks of information. Whole ideas will appear in your head in one go, and you'll be wondering 'Where did that come from?!' Humans are going through a developmental change – it's exciting!

THE NEW CHILDREN

Volunteers from around the galaxy have arrived to assist the new Earth. Sounds crazy? It's real! Bear with me here. High vibrational and pure spirits have chosen to be born into our dense atmosphere here on Earth, because we need help. For too many years we've been leading the planet towards tragedy. We blow holes in the ground, poison the land, and experiment with chemicals and processes we have no right to. Waste is dumped at sea or buried on land, hidden but not forgotten. Wars, riots… what are we doing? It's time to stop. Our extra-terrestrial and inter-dimensional brothers and sisters hold up their hands in horror at the damage we have already done to our precious planet. We will not be allowed to blow ourselves up. Can you imagine the far-reaching effects on other worlds (both seen and unseen by us)? It's not just us who will be affected by the damage! If our Earth explodes, it will affect first our own universe, then our galaxy and then other galaxies – like ripples on a pond. Who knows what damage we have already done to the worlds beyond our own?

Just as in the TV series *Star Trek*, there is a code of non-interference followed by all those from other realms; what could our sky-friends do to help without interfering? They couldn't just appear on the planet – that has been done before and previous generations of humans worshipped these beings as gods. (Look no further than the 'myths' and legends of ancient civilizations to discover when and where this happened.) Everything they taught us was misused – ancient technology was always turned into weaponry by the warrior human races.

They (our soul brothers and sisters from other realms) decided to send in souls in 'human form'; they have been born 'as humans' this time round. It was agreed that this was an acceptable way of making the changes needed to save the planet. These souls enter the body at birth, the same as other souls do. Many of our own children and grandchildren are part of this 'volunteer group'. I wrote about these children in my book *Angel Kids*, if you're interested in finding out more. Even if this sounds far-fetched to you, I feel sure you will sense the truth in what I am saying. This is no new-age mumbo-jumbo!

Numerous parents, carers and teachers around the world have become aware of their children's special abilities. These youngsters seem wise and knowledgeable in ways that others don't. Lots of them have obvious psychic abilities, some simple and some extraordinary. In 1997, a book by Paul Dong and Thomas E. Raffill called *China's Super Psychics* really laid out some of the extremes of the new wave of abilities. Many of these children formed part of the first wave of volunteers, testing the way for others to follow. Some of the people discussed in the book were born with their unusual abilities, others had abilities appear after accidents and illnesses (following a near-death experience or as a result of being struck by lightning, for example). Others developed their abilities through regular deep meditation techniques or through *qi* (energy or life-force) practices such as Qi Gong.

One young girl was able to 'read' written words on pieces of paper zipped inside a pencil case. After seeing the Chinese character for 'yellow dog', she imagined outlining the shape, picturing going over it in her head. When the tester opened the pencil case the character had now been written for a second time on the paper… without the pencil case having been opened. A second test using the Chinese characters for 'high mountain flowing water' produced the same result with a second version somehow being psychically created by the child on the paper using her mind alone! This is mind-blowing, but it's just the beginning.

This story was posted on my psychic children forum:

'My 10-year-old son has had an imaginary friend since he was about three; she's called Gloria and he still chats to her and plays with her. I have always wondered if it's his guardian angel or a spirit. Until a few years ago he used to read my mind and his brother's, and reply to things we were thinking but hadn't said. It used to scare his brother, but I found it fascinating. He also used to describe a little girl at my mother's old house, and funnily enough my Nan, who was psychic but has passed now, described the same little girl. He no longer reads my mind but still has Gloria, his "imaginary" friend.' – HELEN

Researchers at a college in China's Yunnan Province worked with several children to see if they could develop their psychic abilities further. After just one week, the group of five was able to read using their fingers, palms, toes and the soles of their feet. They would run their hands over the paper or stand on the words, absorbing them psychically and being able to translate the 'sense' of the words into actual words… as if they were reading them! How can a human being 'read' by just scanning the words using body parts and not their physical eyes? It seems impossible, yet it happened.

In another experiment, four girls were given flower vases that were sealed inside containers. They were then asked to 'pick' a flower or flower bud (psychically, in their mind's eye) to place in the vase. When the seals were broken to check on the success of the experiment, the girls had each filled the vases as requested. One girl's vase contained a winter jasmine bud, another had a tree leaf, the third had a flower bud and the fourth a flower in full bloom! The test lasted half an hour but even more surprising was the fact that one of the testers noticed something unusual about one of the flower buds. He himself was the breeder of a rare type of tea; he had a plant he'd been growing for three years on his balcony at home and it had produced a single bud. When the tester got home, the bud had gone, selected through the mind power of the psychic child and transported psychically to the vase in the sealed container! Naturally he was both excited by the result and disappointed at his loss!

Other psychic children showed abilities such as being able to open flower buds with their mind alone, bringing them into bloom. In 1993 and 1994 a film crew made a documentary about these psychic abilities called *An Investigation of Life's Extraordinary Phenomena*. According to Paul Dong and Thomas E. Raffill's 1997 book, this documentary became a series and was later made into 13 videos called *Developing the Latent Powers of Children*.

The psychic power of these children is real, tested and proven, and although testing to the same extent seems not to have been carried out in other parts of the world (as far as we are aware), parents everywhere will tell you it's unnecessary – they already know their children are psychic! This next story was also posted by a reader on my website:

'My nine-year-old son has told me that he "knows things" about people, and he sometimes knows what's going to happen before it happens. On meeting new people he instantly likes or dislikes them based on a feeling he gets. He has reported that he sees "funny people" walking around (and I don't mean the neighbours!). I quite often feel the same way, however I have never spoken to him about any feelings I have.' – SUZIE

If you'd like to read more stories like these, you may be interested in my book *Angel Kids*, also published by Hay House.

OTHER CHANGES

People are now returning to exercising and meditation where once they spent their time on pursuits such as watching TV or playing computer games. It's time to start moving our bodies once more, walking instead of taking the car.

Many of my friends have become one-car families instead of the more usual two in my part of the world. More of us are conscious of saving electricity and gas in our homes. When we leave the house we try and remember to unplug our plugs at the socket; did you realize that even if your electrical item is switched off, it will still use electricity if it's plugged in?

More of us remember to recycle or take our own shopping bags to the supermarket, saving millions of pounds on manufacturing plastic bags, as well as the energy saved in production. Can you squeeze out that last bit of paste from the toothpaste tube, or cut the end off your bottle or tube and use up that final blob of cream? Can you wash out and re-use the jam jars? Can you collect seeds in the garden to create new plants?

The recession has taught us many things including how to use less and how to need less. Things that we once thought were important are no longer so. Many recall earlier, leaner times and understand this 'new' way of living very well, having lived it previously. Can you mend instead of throw away? Can you change the colour rather than buy new? Polish shoes, re-spray waterproof coats and sew those buttons back on?

As spirits we need none of the 'comforts' of earthly life... although we certainly have become accustomed to them! As we pass through the gate of heaven we recall that the whole reason for living was not to acquire things or gather wealth; how far off-track we have come!

Why are we here? We live to LOVE; to love one another, to love the animals on the planet, to love the very Earth itself. It's time to fill your mind with positive and loving thoughts. Naturally people who do not resonate at this new higher vibration will fall away. You will no longer feel connected to people of a lower vibration. People who cause you angst and stress will no longer form a part of your world. Let them go with love. What is the meaning of life? LOVE – it's as simple as that.

You'll find yourself more drawn to people who lift you up, and to work that fulfils you. As well as changing your diet you may well find you wish to dress differently, and certainly take better care of your body. Enjoy this journey into a simpler and purer way of living. Fizz and crackle with energy as you re-claim your real self.

ANGELS

And so the angels have come. It's time to awaken to our one true purpose, to recall our missions on Earth. Why are we here? We'll examine this a little more later on, but of one thing I will reassure you, you are not alone. Even if you sometimes feel lonely, know that you are supported by your guardian angel and, at this time, many other beings throughout the universe. Exciting times are ahead, so hang on tight and enjoy the ride!

How to Use This Book

This book is split into three different sections. My readers always love to know what's been happening in my own spooky life, so I'll share a few experiences of my own since I wrote for you last. I meet loads of lovely people in my work so I will concentrate on some of those kinds of experiences in particular! What have I been up to? Read Part One to find out... or you can jump right to Part Two if you prefer.

Part Two is all about angels. What are they? How can you work with them in your own life and what is happening on the planet right now? Of course I know you'll like some fun tips on connecting with your own angels and guides, so I have included a little inspiration for you in this section.

Part Three is full of your real-life angel stories. I remember once a fan picked up a copy of one of my books to take away on holiday with her. A couple of years previously she'd read another of my books and, following this, had e-mailed me to share an angel story of her own. Even though I'd written to tell her I would be including her angel experience in my next book, this woman had forgotten all about it. Imagine her surprise when she came across her own experience by accident in the new book she'd just purchased! When she got back from holiday she immediately wrote to me again. 'Now I know the stories are real,' she explained. 'You wrote up my story exactly as I had shared it with you!' So there you go – the stories are 100 per cent real!

Part 1

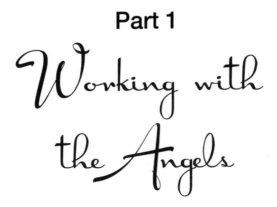

Working with the Angels

'I am near you, can you feel me?
Can you sense my wings around you?
Do you know that I'm beside you?
Can you tell you're not alone?'
Jacky Newcomb

My Psychic Life

*'Millions of spiritual creatures walk the Earth
Unseen, both when we wake and when we sleep.'*
JOHN MILTON, PARADISE LOST

In one way you could say I've been working with the angels my whole life… in another you could simply say that *they* began working with *me* in a serious way about 12 years ago… give or take a bit! Angels have popped in and out of my life over my whole life, really, and my family as a whole has always been a little spooky… especially me!

My sisters and I had paranormal phenomena occur throughout our childhood: deceased relatives were regular visitors in dreams, for example. At first it was just Uncle Eric, Dad's brother, but then many years later when Dad passed on he too became a regular visitor; so much so that my sister Madeline Richardson and I wrote a book about our family's psychic adventures after Dad passed away. Dad, like Eric before him, flickered lights,

3

set off alarms and messed with music playing on the CD player and radio. He was even able to change the TV channel; and, of course, like my own guardian angel, Dad and Uncle Eric also left white feathers as signs that they had been around, reminding me that everything would be OK.

This very week, for example, Dad came to visit. Dad was a big fisherman in life – it was one of his 'signs', if you like. We even hung a set of painted wooden fish on his coffin (with the words 'Gone fishing' written on the side). Dad is always around, but now he was ready with a clever new way of showing me that he was with me…

I've been working on my website (my husband and I build websites), and as usual got carried away with the time. I'd worked literally all night and it was now 7:30 in the morning. I suddenly felt that I was no longer alone, and whispered to an unseen person, 'Yes, I'll just finish this and then I'll go right to bed.' I had just gathered together a selection of magazine covers and was assembling them into one last picture ready to display on the website. I typed in the name of the file, 'magazine montage', and hit the save button. As I looked up at the screen, ready to move my new image into place, I noticed it had been renamed something else. My file was now called 'FISHING'! Even the most sceptical must admit it's not easy to mistype 'fishing' in place of the word 'magazine'! No other files or pictures on my entire computer were named fishing

– I'd not visited any websites by this name, there was no way I could have named my file this way by accident (I have no interest in fishing!). My caller was Dad, of course, visiting from the other side to see what I was up to, and likely wondering why I had stayed up all night! Bless him.

Regular readers will know that this phenomenon – spontaneous afterlife communication – fills many of my books. I love to share real-life stories of angels and the afterlife. Who needs fiction? Real life is far more mind-blowing, isn't it?

Like my other books, this one also contains stories of angel protection and love. I've interviewed many of the people who've shared their stories with me so that we can indulge in a little more background about who the people are and why their stories are so special… I wanted to share the stories behind the encounters.

I haven't stayed on the point of strictly 'angel stories', though; many other dramatic and thought-provoking encounters deserve a hearing, too, so I've mixed them all together for your perusal. I know that you will be moved and stunned, as I have been. Can these stories be true? They are, all of them, real-life encounters from normal, everyday folk just like you and me.

It's exciting to see that other people, too, have begun writing about their angel stories – the craze has really caught on. Over the years, more and more celebrities have reached out to say that they too believe in angels.

Many TV personalities read my books and are happy to talk about their own beliefs in magazines and newspaper interviews. 'I believe in angels…' they admit, or 'An angel helped me to get where I am today…' they suggest, without a hint of embarrassment! What this all means, of course, is that these days it's OK to talk about your angels. It's acceptable to believe in these other-worldly beings. But if you're like me, you already do!

FINE-TUNING… WITH AN 'ANGEL DIET!'

My own journey has taken a real turn this year. Over previous years my angels have suggested politely that I might consider looking at my diet. They wanted me to concentrate on higher-vibration foods: fresh fruits and vegetables, salads, seeds, nuts and high-quality proteins (I don't eat meat but love fish). I began in a half-hearted way – sugar was a big craving for me – but the angels were insistent that I shouldn't be eating it. I needed to be 'lighter' spiritually.

While leaving room for my 'free-will', I suddenly found that foods I had eaten my whole life and enjoyed (cakes, biscuits, sweets… especially chocolate, thick white bread, cream and sugar) were no longer able to stick around in my body. I suddenly found I had a sort of allergy to them. I've also cut right down on salt (my blood pressure reduced as a result). Not that I am complaining – my brain seems clearer for the healthier diet. With very few processed foods entering my body, I've noticed a difference in the way I feel... and look.

The world is changing and we must change with it. Never have we had access to such a wide variety of lovely fresh fruits and vegetables; organic produce has come down in price, and of course many of us can grow our own. Even if all you can manage is a windowbox or a few pots on the windowsill, you can grow fresh herbs to cook with.

Fresh water is still cheaper to drink than pretty well everything else, and it's what our bodies crave more than anything. Headaches and all types of things are caused by dehydration – are you drinking enough water?

Another thing I've been drawn to this year is spirulina, a blue/green algae supplement in tablet form and available from healthfood shops. It's full of iron (useful if you don't eat meat), is almost a 'whole food' and gives me great energy (it easily replaces the sugar I used to eat with the energy boost it gives me). Some manufacturers claim it has other properties, too, but I'll leave you to decide that for yourself. And please do remember to consult with your doctor before making any changes in your diet.

Have I suddenly become a 'health nut'? No! I do stretches and lift some light weights most days, swim once or twice a week and use a gym maybe once or twice a week. I'm getting there! I have lost weight, it's true – a useful side-effect. I still eat chips occasionally and drink the odd glass of champagne… a girl's got to have a little fun, right? We all need to be naughty occasionally (but don't tell anyone I said that!).

IAN LAWMAN BURIED ALIVE

Last year I followed along while my friend, TV medium and exorcist Ian Lawman, was buried alive for charity. Ian 'lived' in a small coffin-shaped box, six feet under in the grounds of the haunted Dudley Castle in the West Midlands. He survived on water and food tablets during his quest, which lasted seven days. Mad? Maybe, but also very brave. Ian was raising money for two great charities: Help for Heroes and PC David Rathband's Blue Lamp Foundation. PC Rathband has sadly since passed away.

While Ian was buried under nearly two tons of soil, I, along with many of his fans, were following along in the live chatroom… it was very addictive and I found myself checking in regularly! Several times a day Ian chatted to fans with the aid of a webcam that was attached to the inside of the 'coffin'. Fans asked questions in the chatroom and a friend at the scene passed on the messages. Ian was able to reply to fans with the help of the webcam, and this was streamed live.

Ian had several paranormal experiences while he was buried underground, including spirits who visited him while he was asleep – did they think he had died like them? Ian was sealed into his box, although he did have a glass tube above his head (also sealed), which meant that he had some subdued natural light coming from above. The whole area of the 'burial' site was covered with a tent and Ian was guarded 24 hours a day by volunteers.

My favourite thing of all, though, was when Ian communicated with me via text (he had a mobile phone with him which he was able to use for occasional text messages to family and friends; no signal for chatting, though). I told Ian that I believed he was being protected by angels during his experience. The very next day, Ian texted me to say that when he woke up he found a white feather stuck to the upper (sealed) side of the glass partition above his head! Even more strange was the fact that this mysterious feather later disappeared. It seems the angels really were watching over him after all. Congratulations on raising so much money, Ian!

ITV'S *THIS MORNING*... ON ANGELS

I was delighted to be invited on to ITV's *This Morning* for a special slot about angels. I love appearing on the show and have done so a number of times over the years. This time I sat alongside TV presenter and angel-believer Gloria Hunniford. Immaculately dressed and lovely as always, we chatted together in the studio about our beliefs and then carried on our conversation in the Green Room afterwards.

Gorgeous presenter Holly Willoughby was pregnant during my appearance and I was delighted to have sourced an angel-teddy (a teddy with angel wings) as a gift for her that I handed over during our segment. Holly went on to have a healthy baby girl shortly afterwards… I hope she liked her teddy!

The feedback on e-mail and on Facebook following the show was phenomenal, and as always I came home with some great photographs as mementos.

…AND GHOSTS

TV medium Barrie John made an appearance on *This Morning* just a couple of weeks later. He was on the show to discuss ghosts. Poor Holly appeared frightened during the segment and at one point actually left the studio. Her co-presenter Phillip Schofield said that he's never had anyone leave during an interview before… and on this occasion it was actually his co-host.

The studio decided they had better get Holly some help, and sent in the professionals: psychotherapists and personal development coaches Nik and Eva Speakman. The couple worked with Holly to desensitize her to her fear of spooky phenomenon and, a few days later, Barrie was asked back to the studio to do the session again. Sadly this time he was unable to appear due to prior commitments, so he recommended that I take his place.

Now, Cornwall is a long way from London. Mum had just arrived from the Midlands for a holiday (a few hours' drive away) but the programme makers were kind enough to accommodate her, too, and with husband John driving the three of us had a fantastic time in the capital. I suggested to Mum and John that they sneak into the studio during my TV appearance. Mum was thrilled at the opportunity of the unexpected London trip… and having her photograph taken with Phillip and Holly was an unforeseen treat! She loved it!

I was delighted to be asked to appear on the show again so soon after my last appearance. This time I was a guest alongside Dr Chris French, whose main research interest is the psychology of paranormal beliefs and paranormal experiences. He was the 'sceptic' and I was the 'believer'. In reality our beliefs are quite similar, so I joked with Chris before the show that we should have a pretend fight on air to make for a more dramatic appearance… we didn't, but as Holly was now cured of her 'phobia' we ended up the four of us having a really good giggle during the segment! Well done, Holly!

MEETING RIGHT SAID FRED

More fun: I was thrilled to have been invited to go to London to see Right Said Fred in concert. Singer Fred Fairbrass is a Facebook friend, and my husband and I set off to spend another night in London. The brothers were amazing and we found ourselves singing along to all their old hits.

Richard Fairbrass and I had exchanged a few messages on Twitter and he told me that they'd once lived in a haunted home. This was fascinating to me. I'm planning on interviewing the brothers soon to discover more about their psychic story; perhaps I'll include it in a future book!

PSORIASIS

Most of us have issues with our health and mine is that I have the skin condition psoriasis. Psoriasis is a skin disease that occurs when the immune system sends out faulty signals that speed up the growth cycle of skin cells. Psoriasis is not contagious but it's very annoying! Certain spots of skin 'renew' more regularly than the rest, which results in copious skin shedding and white 'Smartie-sized' patches of skin dotted along the limbs. This can cause challenges with the type of clothes I wear… sparkly is good as it hides skin flakes! It can be challenging to have this condition when you're in the public eye. The beautiful reality TV star Kim Kardashian and the singer LeAnn Rimes have both spoken about their own struggles with psoriasis.

During a routine visit to my local hospital I was asked to speak to BBC Radio Cornwall about the condition.

I loved the opportunity of discussing psoriasis with the public – anything to help others understand. Many people with psoriasis find themselves lacking in confidence; it's a very debilitating and embarrassing condition. I have found many ways of dealing with it myself – humour being one of them – so I jumped at the chance of speaking openly about it. After the interview the presenter told me, 'That was great, I can see you've done this before…' and I had, although usually I'm talking about the paranormal, of course… little did he know! Shhh!

Please visit my website www.jackynewcomb.com for more information.

…AND GAY RIGHTS!

Shortly afterwards I stayed up late to listen to a friend speak as a guest on talkSPORT Radio. Unfortunately I'd got the timing wrong and missed my friend's slot completely. Strangely enough I had tuned in to a section about gay rights. Listening to a very obnoxious and rude man who suggested that all homosexuals should be shot, I could feel myself getting mad. Are there really so many ignorant people in the world? I couldn't help myself, so I was full of confidence as I rang the talkSPORT studio. My call was put through and of course I wasn't angry on the phone, just the voice of reason! We are all equal in God's eyes, are we not? Live and let live! We humans need to be more tolerant about all types of lifestyles and personal preferences!

So there we go, two unexpected radio interviews… not on my 'usual' subjects, but both worth speaking up about!

CORNWALL TODAY MAGAZINE

When we lived in Staffordshire I was featured a couple of times in the local glossy magazine, *Staffordshire Life*. Naturally I was keen to do the same with the Cornwall county magazine *Cornwall Today* once we had moved to the area.

The lovely Liz Norbury and photographer Charles Frances appeared at my home to do a type of 'at home' feature with my husband John and me. Being prepared, we'd rushed out to the local garden centre and filled the garden pots with flowering plants… just in case any outdoor photographs were needed (a good excuse for more flowers, I thought). The garden looked lovely.

A last-minute photograph of me holding my small black cat Magik was one that made it into the magazine, along with a photograph of me standing by the front door – alongside all my new flowering pots (phew, justified!). John was also featured standing next to his beloved motorbike – the feature complete! We had such a lot of fun and of course there is always way more I want to say than there's room for in a magazine! I can talk about my favourite subject for hours, and love to give readers the opportunity of seeing how an ordinary person can have an extraordinary interest!

BLONDE BOMBSHELL?

A journalist friend of mine gave me a call one day to ask if I would be interested in doing a magazine feature about my hair. 'You've made a dramatic change to your hair, haven't you Jacky?' she asked. Of course I had – I used to be a brunette but now I am a blonde! (You thought it was natural? Thanks!)

I quickly found some old photographs and then searched out some new ones. I know I love those before-and-after shots, so I assumed her readers would, too. I just hoped the readers would like the new look better than the old! It was great to feature in a glossy magazine!

PICTURE THIS

Then in June I seemed to have a houseful of people. My sister Madeline (Richardson) and I, having just written a book together, decided we needed some publicity shots taken. I always like to have nice photographs 'in stock' ready for any magazine or newspaper article that comes my way – because if you don't have your own photograph ready, the publication will send their own photographer. Call me a control-freak if you like, but I prefer to choose my own photographs rather than wait and see what they've gone with!

We called upon a local photographer to come out to my house to take some photographs, both formal and informal. He arrived with a lot of equipment – the white backdrop was going to be way too big to fit into the room, but we had a white window blind ready to hang and use instead. It worked pretty well, but when it was pinned into place it became immediately obvious you could see right through to the doorway underneath. I should not have underestimated our clever photographer, though, as he'd brought along many different lights and reflectors. By the time he had finished you could see almost nothing but a perfectly white, translucent backdrop, which looked exactly like we were posing in a studio.

John took some behind-the-scenes shots with the room full of lighting and wires – it was certainly a lot of fun! After the inside shots we posed in the garden before all piling into two cars and hitting the local woods. By this time the sunlight was streaming through the trees and they filtered the light magically. We did some shots of us both looking up into the air – we captioned them 'looking for faeries' (we didn't find any) as they looked so ethereal! One of these shots is posted on my website. I have a strapless dress on but in the photograph you can only see my bare shoulders – my daughter rang me indignant, 'Mum! You look like you aren't wearing any clothes!' she said. It did make me laugh!

After four hours of posing we were both exhausted but luckily John pulled together a lovely stir-fry for tea. I felt so tired I could barely lift my fork and for the first time really admired the work done by professional models who can keep going all day! My sister Madeline stayed overnight because the following day we had someone coming to film a video of the two of us together. This was to promote another book we had written together. The actual filming took less than an hour, although we'd each taken well over an hour to get ready!

I adore writing but when you first start you never really think about the work that goes on behind the scenes. Photographs, promotions, book-signings, interviews, radio and TV appearances, talks, workshops and building websites… luckily I love it all!

SNOOKER GHOSTS

Talking of book-signing… I had a wonderful time at Walter Henry's Bookshop in Bideford, Devon. I meet such lovely people at these events, and then afterwards we stayed in a lovely B&B. It was like a mini-holiday. The room at our B&B was lovely, really beautiful and on the ground floor of the property – a large, light room with patio doors that led right out into the garden.

To get to our room we had to pass through a room that held a full-sized snooker table. In the middle of the night I was awoken by the very loud sound of snooker balls being hit by a cue. It was really noisy yet, when we went to peek, there was no one in the room, the lights were off and the cover was on the table! I rushed back into bed, but the sound of cue on ball went on for about 4 minutes… it was really spooky!

The next morning I mentioned it to the owners, who nodded sympathetically. Apparently when they had first moved into the house they were awoken by the noise, too, and had come downstairs prepared to tell their young boys to get back into bed and stop playing snooker. Like me, when they got into the room they found it empty, the cover tied securely over the table… and the boys fast asleep in bed!

BECOMING A NANA

The most exciting thing that happened to me this year is that I became a grandmother for the first time. My eldest daughter gave birth to a beautiful little girl on 1 January 2011… a very magical date indeed. I can't tell you her name, I'm afraid (it's a secret!), but I can tell you that she has big beautiful eyes and laughs all the time. I can't wait until she can talk… I wonder if she remembers her past lives or has any words of wisdom for us? These youngsters are so special; all of them are precious miracles. You know of course that I'll let you know if there is anything mystical to report!

Part 2

All About Angels

'Angels are spirits, but it is not because they are spirits that they are Angels. They become Angels when they are sent. For the name Angel refers to their office, not their nature. You ask the name of this nature, it is spirit; you ask its office, is that of an Angel, which is a messenger.'

St Augustine

Your Questions Answered

So here you go, let's investigate everything 'angel'; the who, what, when and why of guardian angels! This is for everyone who is new to the subject and those of you who've been studying the phenomenon for many years. I know you'll discover just a little bit more about our celestial friends here.

Over the years I've created many books on angels and full of angel stories (more about these at the end of the book). The questions people ask me about their angels have evolved, and in some cases become very sophisticated, indicating the increased interest in and knowledge of all things spiritual. I thought it would be wonderful to invite my social networking group (on Facebook) to ask me their own angel question so that I could answer them here for you.

They have come up with questions I would never have thought of, and I've thoroughly enjoyed answering them.

What Does the Word 'Angel' Mean, and Will Angels Accompany Jesus When He Returns?

Let's start at the very beginning. The word 'angel' means *messenger*. They are attendants or guardians of God (Creator); spiritual beings but not souls. Angels are beings of light. They are mentioned in the Hebrew and Christian Bibles and also the Koran. Other religious texts will use the word 'angel' (or its translation) to mean a spiritual being. Angels are intermediaries between God and humankind (a sort of 'middle man' in human terms!).

The word 'angel' can sometimes be used to refer to a human messenger, although in modern-day language this would more likely be a deceased human being. 'Angel' is sometimes used to describe any spiritual entity and also human beings who are angelic (spiritual, loving people, those who help others as an angel might). According to Aristotle, angels are 'pure contingent spirits'.

The second part of the question here is harder to answer. It means we assume or believe in the Second Coming of Jesus. As Jesus is the Son of God, and God is, for me, another word for our Creator, the answer is with

God's will or with God's choosing. I have refrained from using 'him or her' to refer to God, as God is a creating energy rather than a human with gender (neither male nor female).

Where Does the Name 'Angel' Come from?

In Latin we use the word *angelus*, and Greek *angelos*; the English word 'angel' is believed to be a blending of the Old English/Germanic word *engel* and the Old French word *angele*.

Does Everyone Have a Guardian Angel? Do We Have More than One Guardian Angel?

They have! Some of us, depending on our life's work, will have many angels working with us and watching over us. Angels are always with us, waiting to be called upon to assist us, care for us, guide and guard us.

Do They Choose Whom to Watch Over?

Angels are assigned to us rather than choosing us. Humans have free will (freedom of choice) but angels haven't. Their 'will' is the will of God.

Are They Related to Us?

Not if you are using the term 'angel' in the traditional sense to mean messenger of God. Deceased loved ones (relatives and friends who have passed over) do also watch over us (if they choose to) and sometimes they refer to themselves as our 'guardian angels'. By this they mean that if we feel sad or lonely they are aware of this and draw close to us on the Earth side. Many humans now feel, hear and sense their deceased loved ones – I've written about many hundreds of cases relating to this phenomenon.

Do We Have the Same Guardian Angel throughout All Our Incarnations?

Again, this depends on the will of God. These things are decided upon by a Council of Elders, or Divine Council, before we are incarnated on Earth. So again, the answer is yes and no because this same group usually follow all of our lives, but sometimes (depending on the life and its challenges) we would have other angels come in to assist us: 'specialist angels' with specialist skills; in the same way that on Earth if you wanted to learn a foreign language you would seek out a teacher with this skill (of course these talents are varied in the same way that they would be on Earth. The teacher you seek to learn a language from will most likely be different from the one who teaches you to play the violin or to surf!).

Does Anyone Share an Angel?

Sometimes, and especially if we and another have similar interests. Angels can be brought in to teach groups or watch over several people at the same time when they are together on a particular pursuit.

Where Do Our Angels Go? Do They Sit on a Cloud All Day Playing Harps?

Only on greetings cards! Angels don't 'go' anywhere, they just 'are'. Time does not exist as an issue for angels because only on Earth do we work with 'time' in a line (with a beginning, middle and end). Everywhere else, everything exists as 'now'. (Complicated? Yes, I know! But to be fair the answer to this question would probably take a whole book on its own!)

Do Angels Hold Human Form and Walk Among Us?

They can do, but they usually don't. Angels exist on a finer vibration than humans. Think of a cloud or the steam from a kettle – now think finer than that. It's challenging for them to hold human form, but in emergencies they can do so for the briefest time.

Humans have witnessed angels on many occasions. They usually appear in times of great need. As humans we are more likely to see an angel in a human form while we are in an 'altered state' of consciousness (asleep or meditating, for example). Angels can sometimes manifest during illnesses or accidents – they can seem to appear and disappear in an instant.

Do They Connect with Us in Different Ways Depending on What 'Clair' Is Strongest?

I understand by this that the reader is referring to the psychic skills clairvoyance (the psychic skill of clear-seeing), clairsentience (clear-sensing), clairaudience (clear-hearing), etc. Yes, they do connect to humans in many different ways. I will list some of these later on in the book.

Can Humans Become Angels?

Well, not normally (in the traditional sense of the use of the word 'angel'), but if you mean do our deceased loved ones watch over us a little like angels do, then the answer is a definite YES! They can and they do.

In times of trouble or danger, people occasionally hear the voice of a deceased loved one calling out to them in warning. Magic, isn't it?

Do Angels Have Feet or Do They Disappear in Mist or a Cloud?

This is a really interesting question. Angels don't have bodies in the way that humans have. They are actually beings of light, etheric beings (fine and airy) and only show themselves with 'bodies' for the comfort of others. Therefore if they appear, they manifest whatever is needed for us to recognize them (the 'feet' might not be necessary!), which is why not every part of the body is always seen.

How Do Angels Take Care of Their Wings?
(Especially when they leave so many of their feathers on the ground to say they called?)

This question follows on beautifully from the last one. Angels sometimes appear to humans with wings and halos (or bright auras of light) around them. They are light beings – and don't have 'real' bodies in the way that we might understand them. So angels don't actually have or need wings to fly; they manifest them so that we humans know they are angels.

I'll answer the feather question later on.

Do Angels Stay with Us from the Day We Are Born?
When We Pass Over Does Our Guardian Angel
Remain Our Guardian Angel or Do They Become a
Newborn Baby's Guardian Angel?

Yes, angels are usually with us even before we are born, and stay after we pass on. Many who go through a near-death experience actually get to meet their angels, who appear to collect them and take them heaven-side. You can meet your own guardian angel by following along with a guided meditation (details later in the book).

Ask your angel to appear to you in your own meditations, or maybe your angels will even pop into a dream if you ask nicely. Mine do occasionally – usually disguised but with a message. They don't look like the 'normal' angels we think of, and certainly don't appear with wings. In my dreams the angels appear as 'bit parts' in little plays, which they perform to teach me something. It's only when I wake up I realize they were angels!

Do They Move On to Someone Else When We Die and They Have Helped Us to Cross Over?

Again, this depends really on whether we have a need for a guardian at that time. Angels can be in more than one place at one 'time' (human time) so if we need them, or we incarnate again, they can be with us again.

Is There Such a Thing as a Dark or Evil Angel?

The Bible talks about fallen angels, the angels that turned against God. These days the word 'angel' is used to describe a being of light mainly, the good and positive energies. If dark angels still exist we would probably use other words to describe them. Personally I have never come across any.

Since We Have Free Will, When Can Angels Intervene?

Angels prefer to be asked for their help – it's easier for them if we give them permission. You don't need to follow any complicated rituals (unless you want to or you enjoy that sort of thing).

In times of emergency it's natural to call out for help (although often we don't really know whom or what we are calling for). Angels can respond to this call for help and some of the more dramatic rescues and life-saving assistance seem to happen during these times of danger.

You can ask your angels for help with anything or at any time. Do remember, though, that as humans we have been given free will for a reason. It's important that we try and work through our own problems so that we can learn and grow as souls. Why not ask your angel to help you to sort out a challenging situation rather than solve every problem for you? Empower yourself! If you need help then you can ask your angel to send someone to assist you to work out your problem.

Do We Have to Ask Directly?

You can ask in whatever way you feel comfortable. You may prefer to ask God directly to send an angel, or just ask your angels to watch over you and your family – a simple thing you can do every morning at breakfast. You can wear a piece of jewellery that represents your request (a pin or brooch in the shape of an angel, for example) or write your request down in a little notebook. Just do whatever works for you rather than worrying too much about doing it right. If your intent is pure then the message will be received.

...Or Will They Just Come Along to Help Us If We Really Need Them?

Yes, in emergencies they are always with us, but it doesn't hurt to ask them to intervene just the same. Angels come up with all sorts of ingenious solutions! They are very resourceful.

How Do They Work with Us So They Don't Affect Our Karma?

Angels are never meant to affect our karma. The concept of karma originates from Buddhism and Brahmin orthodoxy, but the idea of karma appears as part of other religions, too (even if the word karma itself isn't used). Karma relates to moral behaviour, and although the exact meaning varies slightly from religion to religion, karma refers to our behaviour as part of the circle of life, cause and effect.

We live to learn lessons in the school of life. During our time 'in class' we have to take care not to harm or hurt others, as doing so builds negative karma, which we have to repay in either this life or the next. This is a very simplistic explanation, of course! To build good karma we work to help others.

In each life on Earth we plan lessons; difficult times sometimes teach us more than easy times. Each problem we overcome or situation we work through creates a 'learning' for the soul. If angels intervene too much (i.e. solve our every little problem) as humans we would learn nothing!

Yet humans sometimes feel overwhelmed by their life challenges – even if we don't believe we have created them on some level! Angels can certainly ease the burden by walking beside us, as a really good friend would do. Angels can be an ear to listen and a hand to hold. There is no karma issue with that now, is there?

Can a Guardian Angel Ever Become an Archangel?

This is another 'with God's will' question, but I don't see why they would; although I'd never say *never*!

Can a Master Ever Become an Angel?

An 'ascended master' is a spiritually enlightened being who has evolved from a normal human soul. Jesus is said to be an ascended master. Others you may have heard of include Sanat Kumara, the Buddha, Maitreya, Confucius, Mary (mother of Jesus), Kwan Yin, St Germain, Kuthumi and others. If God chooses they could become angels, but it seems unlikely that a human soul would transfer (normally) to an angelic being. We have our own spiritual path to follow.

How Do I Get My Loved Ones and My Guardian Angel to Come Around Me When I Need Them Most?

The answer is that your angel is always around you. If you want a sign that they are close, then do ask for one – then stay alert. Angels bring many signs, and later on in the next chapter I will discuss some of these in more detail.

Why Don't Angels Appear to Everyone? Why Can Only Some People Feel Them and See Them?

Most people don't see angels – not when they are conscious, anyway. It's really related to the human body's limited ability to perceive them. Our eyes just can't see that range of light. Angels communicate in whatever way they can, and this will mainly be through signs, touch (the sensation of someone holding your hand or laying a comforting hand upon your shoulder), or by bringing help to you or helping to solve a problem in a 'miraculous' way. (See the next chapter for more on this.)

What Do Angels Look Like?

They can appear in whatever way they wish, but most people, on the very rare occasions that they do see angels manifest, tell me they appear as human-type figures without gender (nether male nor female), usually draped in some sort of cloth (a wrap) as clothing, surrounded by bright light. They can appear with or without wings. It is usual for them to be very tall, but sometimes they appear at human height.

Signs from Above

*'Make yourself familiar with the angels and behold
them frequently in spirit; for without being seen,
they are present with you.'*
St Francis de Sales

Now let's look at some of the many signs that angels
bring to let humans know that they are around us. If
you are aware of the signs, you are less likely to miss
them. Over the years I have collected loads of different
types, and even if you are familiar with some, I am sure
there will be a few new ones here for you to enjoy.

Your deceased loved ones (as 'guardian angels' in
their own way) will also use these exact same signs to
show you that they are watching over you. These signs
bring great comfort and joy to all who receive them.

SIGNS FROM THE ANGELS

White Feathers

One of the more common signs of the existence of an angel is the gift of a white feather. I'm sure you will have heard of this one! When you need reassurance, ask your angel for a feather sign. Over the years people have shared extraordinary stories of angel feathers manifesting at the most unusual of times and in the most unusual of places.

'I've recently moved house, and things have gone from bad to worse. My health isn't great, and my little girl has spent three weeks in hospital with a broken arm.

'As I was going through my boxes, a small picture of my granddad dropped to the floor. I immediately felt comforted as I picked it up and said, "Hi Granddad, love you," then I carried on with my busy day. About half an hour later I came back to the spot where I'd found my granddad's picture, and to my amazement there was the most beautiful big white feather just lying there. I've never found a feather before; usually I see butterflies when I'm thinking of Granddad, but this time he came to me (or maybe it was my angel) in a different way.' – LISA

One woman had an angel feather appear from the roof of a lift; another had an angel feather appear just moments after she had vacuumed a room in a house with no feather bedding and all the windows closed. Another lifted a cup and saucer to discover a feather nestling underneath. One woman found a feather (bright pink this time!) inside a sealed plastic shopping bag at a supermarket. The list goes on and on. Where will you find your white feather?

Angel feathers are the ultimate of angel signs. They can be waiting for you on the seat of your car, or lying between the pages of a book. Feathers can be small and fluffy like those from the tiniest baby bird, or big and curled like those from a swan. They come in all sizes, but usually the gift is in their unexpected appearance. Don't worry if your feather is a variation on the usual white variety – coloured feathers do have subtly different meanings but they all still mean, 'We are with you, we are watching over you.'

Angel feathers can be great gifts for those in trouble. Passed-over loved ones can bring a white feather as a present for a grieving relative. Collect the feathers and hand them out to friends in need. They lift the soul immediately. They are so simple, but the best gifts usually are… right? If you are lucky enough to find a lot of angel feathers, why not carry some around in your purse? The angels will show you people who need a little help and support. You too can be an angel and share these loving signs with people in their time of need. Just simply and quietly hand them over.

'While I was on holiday I'd been reading an angel book. I decided to ask my own angels for a sign, and the following day this beautiful little white feather came floating down and I managed to catch it. Little did I realize that on the same street on the opposite side was a little restaurant/bar and it was called "Angel's Bar" and the sign was of two cherubs and angels. I bought back an angel trinket box and a carved angel candle to add to my collection, and my feather is inside the trinket box on my shelf!' – SARAH

Bells and Chimes

After my father and uncle passed away they were regular bell-ringers in the house – doorbell-ringers! If their name was mentioned they both at different times would alert us to their presence. We always checked at the door but no one was there. So concerned were we at one point that one of us would check at the window while another of us rushed to the door! If the doorbell rang, we wondered if it wasn't just a child's prank? It wasn't.

'I have regular contact from my loved ones in spirit, so at a church remembrance mass I asked them for a really big sign that they were there with us. Immediately the fire alarm was set off and I had to try and hide my smile for the rest of the service.' – AMY

Over the years I've collected many stories of spirits and angels setting off alarms and smoke detectors. As well as being a wonderful sign from the other side, it can also be good fun… and annoying in turn. If this type of sign occurs to you and you are not comfortable with it, then ask your angels to stop and they will. Personally I love the humour that comes with it!

'Twelve years ago we heard a long ring on our doorbell in the early hours of the morning. The next day I was told my dad had died.' – ANITA

Flickering Lights

This is another phenomenon that I am personally very familiar with. Usually you will sense the presence of an angel (often a feeling of great peace will come with the flickering). Sometimes another type of sign occurs at the same time. Your angel might also be a deceased loved one who is trying to communicate with you.

I've had fun with this where a family spirit visitor was able to flicker the lights at will, enabling us to have a conversation involving yes/no flicker answers! I'll admit this one can be a little frightening if you are on your own, though. You can ask for this sign if you specifically want it to occur or, as for all the other signs, ask for it to stop if it frightens you.

'My brother turns my kitchen lights on and off; this happened shortly after he died, the first time after me asking him to do so. He didn't do it instantly I asked, so I sat

reading my book and about 10 or 15 minutes later one went off. This continued for a couple of weeks and it was always the same light.

'Then one night I said, "Yeah, if it's really you, why only that light?" A few minutes later it was a different light. People say it's a fault with the wiring, but it's been happening now for nearly three years, and when my mum and dad come to my house the lights are on/off, on/off like he's acknowledging that they're there. I know it's him, nobody can tell me otherwise.' – KAREN

Clockwork

I'm not sure how our angels are able to manipulate any type of clockwork items, but they do. Some of the earliest signs I came across at the beginning of my career involved watches that stopped at the exact time that the wearer/owner, or a loved one of the owner, passed over. It's a classic afterlife sign of continuing awareness after death.

The more modern versions include setting off music boxes that haven't been wound up, winding up clocks that haven't been wound by human hands, and messing with children's toys. Some people have shared experiences of toys that talk in answer to questions they have posed… I can see why this would be spooky! Even though we want a sign, unexplained phenomenon can be quite startling when you are on your own (which is why many of these signs are subtle). As you get used to contact in this way, though, I promise it does get less scary and you'll request it more and more.

This week my bedroom door somehow locked itself from the inside. No one was in the bedroom; my husband had to open the door from the outside with a screwdriver! My signs can be funny… if not a little silly!

Clockwork items that haven't worked for many years can be adjusted and set off by our spirit friends, so do be on the lookout for this type of experience.

'I have a wind-up musical angel globe. The day after I lost my 21-year-old son, Shane, I was lying on the sofa and my younger son was sitting on the floor with a friend. All of a sudden the music started playing by itself. Nobody had touched the globe. We all looked at each other and said, "Shane?" I believe he was letting us know he was OK and had arrived OK.' – FIONA

Birds

The range of bird contact from the other side is vast: hummingbirds in one country and robins in another. Unusual birds (or those favoured by the deceased) can appear on cue, especially following the request for a sign. These birds appear to be very friendly.

'After my father passed over a bird used to tap on the window while I was sitting on the sofa! I wondered what was happening at first! Every day without fail it would come!' – SHARON

My husband John had a baby bird sit between the windscreen wipers of the car last week. It just peered through the window for the longest time and didn't appear afraid at all. It was so unexpected that I picked up my smartphone and took a couple of photographs of the cheeky chappie.

'My adopted son and I went to tend to his mum's grave. A robin landed on her name plaque in front of us and stayed for our whole hour-long visit. It didn't move as we worked, and then near the end it flew to the tree next to us. When we asked it to fly back to the name plaque it did so immediately, it was if it was her saying hello. We then asked three more times and the bird followed our instructions each time!' – LISA

Among the reported phenomena is: a wild bird coming into the house, birds hopping up onto a table or chair where you are sitting, or even a bird sitting on the palm of your hand. You might have a visit from a particular type of bird for several days running following the loss of a loved one. They can tap on the window, as if in greeting, or sit alongside you in companionship while you carry out jobs in the garden or sit reading in the park.

Watch out for groups of birds that usually fly alone, or appear on a specific birthday or anniversary as a 'Hello, we remembered' sign. This next story is particularly special.

'My gran told me that when my granddad died she
had seen a robin on a headstone near the grave during
the burial. When Gran died I saw a robin on the same
headstone during her funeral. Three years later my mum
passed over, and during her funeral both my dad and I
saw three robins sitting together on the same headstone!'
– TRACEY

Butterflies

Butterflies are renowned for appearing in funeral cars
and at wakes. I've even seen them fly right down into
a grave after the loss of a loved one. Watch out for
butterfly signs if you've lost someone.

'I used to work at Windsor Safari Park, where "misting"
the butterfly house was my job. One butterfly always
landed on my shoulder and some days it would be there
most of the day. They have such short lives it left an empty
feeling when one day it wasn't there.

'I searched for over an hour before I found it and cried
the rest of the day. I buried it but thought of it every day for
a long time. I dreamed about it the night before I found out
I was pregnant, and now have three butterfly tattoos, one for
each of my children. That butterfly never complained at my
tears and listened without contempt, for the day before that
butterfly took to landing on my shoulder my granddad had
died, although it took three days for the news of his passing
to reach me.' – NATASHA

I particularly love this fun story, too.

'My mum always said she would return as a butterfly to watch us after she passed away. She died in the December and we were all supposed to be going to a pantomime together. We decided we would still go because we didn't want to upset the children. On the stage, every time a certain actor came on, a butterfly would come onstage, too (a real one)! It had the audience roaring with laughter, considering it was December and not a time for butterflies! To this day I still say Mum didn't want to miss out on the evening out that she'd planned with us.' – **MARYANN**

Rainbows

We're all familiar with this most beautiful of gifts, which never fails to delight. A rainbow is an arc of concentric bands of the colours of the visible spectrum of light. It's created by the refraction and reflection of the sun's rays in water droplets (raindrops, spray or mist, for example – you can get a similar effect by using a hosepipe in the garden on a sunny day, or watching a waterfall with the sun behind you!).

A rainbow shows a continuous spectrum of colours, yet the colours that we see are only the seven colours identified by Isaac Newton (red, orange, yellow, green, blue, indigo and violet). Rainbows have gaps between the colours (not evenly spaced) where other colours exist... colours our human eyes cannot perceive! Fascinating, right?

Double rainbows are rare and are caused by a double reflection. The space in between a double rainbow is called 'Alexander's band' after the scientist Alexander of Aphrodisias, who first described the phenomenon. The second rainbow has a reversed colour sequence (the colours are the opposite way round on the second arc). The air below the rainbow is nearly always brighter than the air above it. Despite the 'science bit', which I thought might interest you, rainbows are so magical and totally tied up with afterlife and angelic contact.

'Last Monday evening my two Saudi Arabian students and I saw an upside-down rainbow above us in the garden. It must have been there 20 or 30 minutes and was brighter than a normal rainbow. There'd been no rain that day either. We Googled it on the computer and discovered they are very rare in the UK and are usually seen only in the Arctic. How lucky were we?' – CAROL

Upside-down rainbows of this type are known as a 'circumzenithal arc', and the sky has to be clear of rain/ low-level clouds for it to be seen. Sunlight shines at a particular angle through a wispy type of cloud (at a height of around 20,000 feet) to create the phenomenon.

I once personally witnessed a rare circular version of this type of 'rainbow', which is not really a rainbow at all. The circular band of colours sat in the sky above our car, and I even managed to get a photograph of this magical

phenomenon. This rare sight is also called a 'sundog' and it happens when low sun catches the vapour of ice crystals in the atmosphere; this is what creates the halo effect. It was quite breathtaking! Of course, all rainbows are miracles and they make wonderful signs from heaven.

On the morning of my dad's funeral a beautiful bright rainbow appeared right over the top of the bungalow where my parents lived. All the family saw it and it felt like a real sign from the other side.

'I visited my mum's grave last month with a friend. I told my friend to look out for a rainbow when we went as it's a common sign for me. Sure enough, the best rainbow he'd ever seen appeared… I knew it would!' – **HEV**

Telephones

One of the first signs my dad brought us after he passed was to ring two mobile phones that had been switched off. On another occasion after my niece had won a prize for work at the local college, my sister's mobile phone rang with a text message (and a little '1' in the box to say a text had arrived). Nothing extraordinary there, until you consider that Dad had been gone for over three years when he 'sent' the message.

Incidentally there was no actual message, but the fact that the phone had brought up his photo, which was still in the phone, was more than enough for us! It just goes to show how our loved ones continue to watch over us from the other side of life, taking an interest in what we are up to. Just this week at a book-signing, a lovely woman came over for me to sign her book and she shared an experience of her own where a relative had telephoned her (while she was fully awake) with the message, 'I'm OK, don't worry about me'. How fantastic is that?

They sometimes use humour, too.

'At my mam's funeral there wasn't a dry eye in the house after I'd read the poem I had written for her; even the priest had tears in his eyes. But then, as we all prayed in silence, my friend's mobile started ringing, I couldn't believe she'd forgotten to switch it off. Funnily enough, the ringtone was the song "Spirit in the Sky"! It wasn't funny at the time, but we do laugh about it now!' – ELEANOR

Sometimes a house phone will ring in the night when no one is on the other end of the line. The ringing usually coincides with a special birthday or anniversary, or it might indicate news of a passing or the anniversary of a passing. The telephone call can also form part of a dream where the deceased loved one is ringing to let you know they have made it safely to heaven. These 'dream' visitations are always clear and vivid, and the dreamer is always fully lucid and aware.

'I had to buy a new mobile phone one Christmas because the screen broke on my old one. I travelled to several towns

looking at phones until I saw one I felt drawn to. I bought it and charged the battery.

'The first time I turned it on I got a text, yet I hadn't given anyone the number and I didn't even know what my own phone number was at the time! I thought it would just be a welcome or sales message from the mobile provider, but when I read it I got quite a surprise. It said, "Merry Christmas and Lots of Love, John and Tzar!" John is my beloved soulmate in heaven and his heavenly companion is called Tzar! Coincidence? I don't think so!' – KAREN

Things Being Moved, Appearing and Disappearing

Another common sign has the potential to be annoying and also funny. Small objects (jewellery, crystals, etc.) can appear and also disappear. Sometimes the object may not have been seen for a very long time when it just turns up right in the middle of the carpet you've just vacuumed. It's always magical when something special turns up, as in this next experience.

'My gran used to burn candles when she was alive. One day after she died I picked up the smell of candles from her room. When I went up there I discovered a letter she had written to my mum. The funny thing is I had been in her room a number of times since she died and I cannot remember seeing that letter before then!' – TRACEY

Photographs and objects that belonged to the deceased can move or fall over. Pictures of loved ones have the habit of wandering backwards and forwards along a shelf, turning themselves around to face the wall or simply flying off the wall!

'My sister found a photo of my mum on the living room floor shortly after her passing in November! My other sister found a message written in condensation on her bedroom window around the same time, and I had a very vivid dream visitation from her. Mum was definitely trying to get through to us.' – CLARE

Here is another mind-blowing experience from Eleanor.

'My friend and I were having a coffee around a year after my mam had died. We were chatting away putting the world to rights, when we heard an almighty crash; at the same time the house phone was ringing. I answered the phone to some really bad news: my little nephew had died. After the call I went to look at what the noise had been, and my mother's picture, which had been hanging on the wall upstairs, had fallen and the glass smashed into bits. The strange thing was that the hook that held it up on the wall was still in place; no windows or door were open, either. The only explanation was that it was a warning of bad news... from my mam.' – ELEANOR

I think that sometimes, after such tragic news, these experiences have a second meaning: it's a way of reminding you that life is eternal and in this case that Eleanor's mum was reminding the family, 'Look, I am here to look after the baby,' and 'Try not to worry, he is safe with me.'

Finally, this one is completely bizarre and was also very confusing to experience, as Eleanor explains.

'One day my friend and I decided to pop to the local shops. We were out for ages, and when we returned I opened the front door to find my loaf of bread (which I always keep inside my bread bin in the kitchen) was on the step in my hallway! It seemed so strange and we both wondered how the bread had got there all by itself. We were still trying to figure it out when the phone rang. I answered it and a woman asked if she could speak to Alice. Well, Alice is my dead mother's name, so I told the woman she must be mistaken; no one called Alice lived at my house. The woman was insistent: "Yes," she said, "I just had a call from this number from a woman called Alice saying she was locked in the house!" Apparently this Alice had sounded very distressed. Well, we were completely baffled. I always wondered if it was my mother coming to visit.' – **ELEANOR**

Mirrors

My sister has seen Dad in the mirror on more than one occasion. This form of communication spooks me a little and I make a point of not looking in the mirror if I wake to go to the bathroom in the night… just in case!

It is traditional in some countries that mirrors in the house belonging to the deceased (or where the wake is held) are covered during the wake to guarantee that the soul does not become trapped! In some countries this even goes so far as to cover all reflective surfaces – it makes you wonder where these customs come from, doesn't it? Maybe in the long-distant past a poor spirit tried to appear in a mirror to reassure a loved one that they were safe…

I posted a request on my social networking site to see if any of my friends had afterlife contact via either mirrors or computers. The following reply came right back (strange coincidence… or was it?!):

'My computer has just shut down and my husband has just this second rung me to ask me which mirror I wanted for our bathroom… Ooooh, spooky!' – LISA

Beautiful Flower Scents

Angels often appear on a cloud of perfume. Common are the strong scents of flowers and vanilla. This can be especially powerful right after a passing or even at the funeral itself (especially if there are no flowers in the room or house you are in at the time).

'My husband's aunt died and she had pretty much brought him up. Then one day we were sitting there and I was overcome with the scent of flowers, and I said to my husband "Come here quick" and he welled up with tears. He said it was the scent of his auntie's favourite flowers.

'A couple of days later in the morning he had a shower and went into the bedroom and was overcome with the smell

again. He said out loud, "Auntie, is that you?" and the lights went on and off twice. It was lovely.' – JOANNE

Just occasionally people pick up the scent of 'not so nice' smells associated with those who have passed… cigarettes and tobacco! Dad used to smoke a lot in his early years, then later when he was meant to have given up he used to carry mints around in his pocket and use these to cover the smell of the occasional misdemeanour. After he passed on, my daughter picked up the strong scent of cigarettes and mints at the same time. She was abroad at the time and I was at home feeling very sad and sorry for myself. She instinctively knew that it was a sign for me and sent me a text on her mobile phone! It really cheered me up. Here is another story.

'I once picked up the smell of mint and I immediately thought of my cousin Susan, who was very ill at the time… 20 minutes later I had a phone call to say Susan had passed away. I can remember my cousin's house always smelling of mint, as she loved to cook with it.' – TERESA

Angels and Music

Angels actually create their own music. The sound of the celestial choir is one of the most beautiful sounds you will ever hear. Imagine beautiful harps and voices in complete harmony. The sound moves you and even has a feel to it. You'll know you are surrounded by complete and unconditional love and peace… magical. Once you have this experience you'll never forget it.

'Three years ago my husband was working away in Denmark and the company he works for was going through a tough period and announced redundancies via the post. Unfortunately, I had to open the letter and let him know over the phone that he had been selected for redundancy. It wasn't a great time for me, with him being away, and I got very upset.

'During my upset I heard music, a sort of fanfare and it was loud and clear. It made me feel very calm. I knew then that everything would be all right. Hubby and his colleagues were flown home and then informed that there had been a mistake and that they were all actually safe and would keep their jobs!' – **BECKIE**

I loved this next experience, too. Music, like colour and all sound, is just another vibration. Do you need to hear it in order to experience it? Maybe not!

'I haven't exactly heard angel music, but I have felt it. I know that sounds strange! It was when I was really upset one day. I was sniffling away in my misery when I was suddenly engulfed in vibrations that made me stop crying. It was as if a thousand beautiful voices had passed through me… and the thing is I actually hadn't heard a thing, but I knew I would be OK and I was safe. It sounds so bizarre but it was so real.' – **JOANNE**

Knocking, Rapping and Similar Phenomena

In my opinion, this section of phenomena is probably the scariest of all, and is often reported as signs from ghosts as well as angels and deceased loved ones! Although many ask for solid experiences, when they happen it can be more than a little spooky! Knocking on the walls and windows has been reported as a warning or advance notice from loved ones as they cross over. They often create this type of phenomenon just to say 'Hi' from heaven.

'When my brother died we had knocking on the windows. We don't get it as much now [because we believe] he is too busy where he is.' – TARA

Another phenomenon that fits into this category includes waking up to find the bed shaking or the covers being removed! Now I know that wouldn't be the type of sign *I* would like to receive. Sometimes these types of tricks can be funny or just heart-warming though, as this story illustrates very well.

'My sister wanted my granddad at her wedding and said as she went down the aisle, "I wish he was here." Just as she got to the altar the door behind the registrar burst open! My sister, my mum and I fell about laughing. It seems like Granddad made it to the church after all!' – NATASHA

Coins

There is a song about 'pennies from heaven', and it's true. Our angels bring us little gifts in the form of pennies from the other side, as well as other small coins. Sometimes the coins are given as a tangible sign that our angels are with us, protecting and comforting us.

'I had to leave my rabbit at the vet's for surgery and was really upset and asking the angels to take care of her. When I stepped out of my car at the vet carpark I found a coin right by my feet. It felt like a sign and I felt much calmer – and my rabbit got through the surgery.' – CORINNE

For some reason my angels bring me the small silver five-pence pieces instead! Five-pence pieces are said to be gifts from the Archangel Michael! It seems I'm not the only one.

'My gorgeous angels leave me five-pence coins everywhere, I have lots… and I find them in the strangest places!' – JOANNE

Dreams

One of the more powerful ways that your angels can appear to you is in a dream. The angel might manifest as just a face in a glowing light, or you might see a full-bodied form appear in front of you. You might know that you are asleep but at the same time be fully aware, or maybe you are just falling asleep or on the verge of waking up.

Your angel might be your guardian, or maybe a deceased relative. Both can use this special way of reaching out from the other side of life.

'I was having a dream, and my uncle was with me. We were in a car and I was driving along a country road with very, very vivid colours on the leaves and the grass, and I could see this even though we were passing very fast. He then said, "Well done on passing your test, Titch," and smiled. The thing is, I knew in the dream he was dead.

'Then the car stopped and he got out and I went to follow him but he told me I couldn't go. He disappeared into a bright light and I woke up. I hadn't actually taken my test when I had the dream, because my test was the following morning. Uncle was right, I passed!' – Lisa

Light and Twinkles

Not every angel appears in full-bodied form. It might be easy to miss flickering and sparkling twinkles of light that appear when you're in need of a little comfort. The lights can appear like glitter in sunshine... a beautiful sign indeed!

'I always see blue lights in my bedroom. I started seeing more of them and more often when I was pregnant, and now that my baby has been born I find it very comforting

and believe it's a sign that my grandparents and the angels are watching over my family.' – **KIM**

Voices

I was once awoken with the word 'test' spoken very loudly in my ear! It makes me giggle even now when I think of it. I was all excited at the time because I figured my angels were going to use this easy method to communicate with me from then on... they didn't! Ha ha. Another time (years later) I was awoken again with the sound of a voice, and this time it was calling my name.

'My son Shane was a joker; if he saw me in town he would sneak up behind me and make me jump, or put his hands over my eyes from behind so I had to guess who it was. Not long after he went "home" I was lying in bed nodding off when all of a sudden I heard a loud whisper really close to my ear, "BOO!" Well, I tell you I jumped out of my skin!' – **FIONA**

Angels and deceased loved ones will mainly use this method of communication in emergencies. I believe it's one of the harder forms of contact for them to achieve. They save it for times when we are in danger, most commonly when driving the car. Many of my readers have written to tell me they heard a voice tell them to stop, slow down or, as in my case, hear their name called, which has woken them up in time to protect them from some hazard!

TOUCHED BY AN ANGEL

Although it's hard for angels to manifest physically in our space, they can sometimes bring the weight of a hand holding your hand or a comforting arm across your shoulder in times of need. Strangely this happens a lot when we are daydreaming, so at times when you are doing boring tasks, this is when you're most likely to experience this phenomenon.

'I was touched by a hand once… or perhaps I should say the hand tried to hold on to me, but it slipped away (even though I couldn't see anything). The next day I found out a friend of mine was killed during the exact hour I'd had the experience.' – SHAYNA

SIGNS THROUGH BABIES AND CHILDREN

Children and small babies often bring us signs that a loved one or an angel is around. Have you ever seen little ones smiling and giggling at 'no one' in particular? Toddlers will point out an angel, even if they can't describe it easily. Little ones will tell you how Grandma came to say goodbye when they were asleep the night before.

Youngsters will regularly keep in contact with deceased family members, even if they've never met them in life. Great-grandparents seem eager to pop back to Earth to meet their new baby relatives. If you are interested in this phenomenon, you'll find stories like these in my book *Angel Kids*. It seems that not all 'imaginary' friends are make-believe!

'I was babysitting my granddaughter, who at the time was about 18 months old, when her talking/singing "Barney the Dinosaur" toy kept going off. If it wasn't that, it was her melody ball toy! She was sound asleep. At the time she had started talking to an imaginary friend and an old man!' – SUSAN

Televisions

If you've ever wondered who's messing with the remote or recorded the wrong channel, you might want to look further than your living family. Angels love to bring us signs through the television, although it can be a little scary when you walk into the room and the television switches on all by itself! Yes, I've had this happen, too!

'My TV switched itself on in the night with the words "Happy Birthday" and balloons on a yellow screen. It was about two weeks after my birthday and my brother had died on my birthday… this year! I know it was a message acknowledging what had happened. When I went to grab my camera to take a photograph, it switched back off.' – KELLY

Radios and Other Music Players

Spirits love to play 'their song' for you on the radio when you're feeling low. That special song, which meant so much to you both, might be playing in a shop you walk into, or start playing on the radio. The tune might be an old one that you just never hear played nowadays, yet if you need to hear the song it starts to play just when you are ready for that reassuring sign.

The sound might unexpectedly increase in volume or go quieter to get your attention, or a particular song might be playing and suddenly stop midway through to be replaced with one more relevant to your feelings.

'My friend's partner died at 29, unexpectedly and traumatically. A year later she was still questioning how she would move on and be with anyone else; she was convinced that her dreams of motherhood and married life were now just dreams.

'At the time we were discussing this we were getting ready to go out for a meal. All of a sudden her iPod randomly started playing one of her partner's favourite party songs! I'm pleased to say she has now met someone and is moving on (albeit slowly) with her life.' – ANONYMOUS

Posters and Adverts, Messages in Print

I remember once asking my angels for a sign; I was driving at the time. I was mulling over my question when I drove over the top of a hill and there in front of me was a massive advertising poster with the word 'YES' in large capital letters. I got my angel answer loud and clear! An author friend of mine had a similar experience.

'The night I gave up my job to concentrate on my writing full time, the bus I was on drove past a 20-foot high poster that said "BELIEVE". That put a smile on my face!' – JANE

Try this one and ask your angels for a sign in a poster or advert. You might pick up a magazine and a picture will give you your message, or maybe like me your sign will come in an advert… sometimes you can be reading a passage in a book or magazine when particular words will almost jump out at you. You get a gut instinct or a strong feeling of excitement in the pit of your stomach when your sign appears. You'll know by how you feel that this is your sign!

Watch out for signs on car bumper stickers, and even car number plates.

Clouds, Bubbles, and More

Have you ever laid down in a field on a summer's day and looked up at the clouds and seen pictures waiting for you? Sometimes a particular shape reminds you of an old dog you used to have, an angel or even the face of someone who has passed on. Our angels love to bring us signs this way, and people have even told me about seeing similar shapes in things like bubbles and candle wax! Maybe your loved one will bring you a sign in this lovely, gentle way.

'One day I saw my mam's face in the clouds. Mam wasn't ill, well I thought she wasn't at the time. Strangely when I told her what I'd seen, her reply was, "That's because I'll be in the clouds tomorrow!" She died the next day.' – ELEANOR

WHEN IS A SIGN NOT A SIGN?

Of course, not every bleep, buzz or flicker is a message from heaven, so it's important to remain sensible and logical, too. Potentially paranormal signs often have normal explanations. I think this story perfectly illustrates this.

'I had constant flickering lights in my new home. I couldn't figure it out; they were flashing fast and furious off and on for weeks. I got it into my head that it must be an angry spirit and I was so convinced that I called in my priest to bless the house. Annoyingly, the light-flickering continued after the blessing, and a friend suggested I call in the electricity company to check it out. How stupid did I look when I discovered that the house had a doorbell for the deaf, so when visitors rang the doorbell, the lights flashed!' – JUDY

Priceless!

Angels and Archangels

'And suddenly there was with the angel a multitude of the heavenly host, praising God, and saying, Glory to God in the highest, and on Earth peace, good will toward men.'
Luke 2:13–14

Let's have a little look at how all the different angels interact with humankind. Then I'd like to tell you a little about the archangels and how they can help us, too. We are most familiar with the guardian angels, those that work closest to humankind, so let's start with them.

GUARDIAN ANGELS

Guardian angels have been around at least since the beginning of humankind – and likely a lot longer than that. Guardian angels are a creation of God, and their roles are specifically to care for and watch over their human charges. They awaken our consciousness to our creator and are our link to the highest energies. As humans the reach to the vibrationary heights of our creator seems impossibly 'far away'; angels act as a sort of intermediary between us and the divine spirit.

Our guardian angels are neither male nor female, although they do sometimes appear as one or the other when seen by humans. They can seem more feminine if gentle and soft energies are appropriate, or more masculine if strong physical characteristics are required. Their appearance can vary depending on our own expectations, too; the angels will adjust how they look to make us feel safe and comfortable.

'I believe my guardian angel saved my life, although I never saw or heard her. I was at work and suddenly had the urge to move from where I was standing; just as I moved away, a pile of wardrobe doors fell over and crushed the table and all my boxes in my work area!' – STEPHANIE

Although angels act on behalf of our creator, they do not expect us to pray to them in the same way that we would pray to God. Your angel's primary role is to offer protection and guidance, love and comfort. It's important that you ask for their help, though, since they are not allowed to interfere with our choices. Humans have 'free will', which means we are permitted to make all our own decisions about what we do, both good and bad. Part of our lessons on Earth is to make the best choices all by ourselves, but the angels can still take care of us when we need it most – as in this next experience!

'In 1999 when I was 19 I had my first ectopic pregnancy. I was 30 minutes away from dying when I was taken to the operating theatre. I remember lying in hospital and I was suddenly being drawn towards this large tunnel. A bright light opened up and on either side was a line of stunningly beautiful angels. I travelled down the tunnel and got towards the end, where a "larger than life" angel was waiting. It spoke to me and said, "It is not your time…" and at the same time I could hear a man calling my name. There was a flash of light and before I knew it I was back in bed. The man was my dad, calling me back to my body.

'That was my first experience with angels, but by no means my last. Ever since my dad called out to me in my left ear, I have been able to hear angels talking, and angel music from time to time. I feel so privileged.' – JOANNE

The New Testament speaks frequently of angels, and references can be found to them all the way through, especially in relation to Jesus. Our angels love us unconditionally – no matter what we do, no matter where we go or what we say. They never judge us, never look down on us. If you listen you will 'feel' their guidance (rather than hear or see it). Of course it's up to us whether we listen or not!

Angels can do many things; let's have a look at some of them:

- take care of loved ones

- watch over our pets

- help keep us safe (remember we also have the responsibility of taking care of ourselves, so it's no good putting yourself in danger and then blaming it on your guardian angel if things go wrong). Ask for your angel to help you – of course they will always step in to save our lives… if it's not our time to die

'My guardian angel showed himself to me when I was almost killed by my mother as a child. He smiled and made me feel safe and loved. My mother suddenly let go of me and left the room. I feel he came because it wasn't my time to die.' – TINA

- comfort us when we feel sad

- support us in times of stress

- keep us calm

'I'd just passed my driving test and was caught in December's snow storm on my own at night. I had to drive seven miles home and was panicking as I couldn't see the road markings or the kerb on the dual carriageway. All of a sudden a sense of calm came over me and from the back seat I heard a voice say, "It's going to be OK," and it was.' – TINA

- bring in help in the form of 'human' assistance

'My angel was an old gentleman who came to my rescue when I was attempting to cross a zebra crossing with my youngest child. It was back in 1990/91 when the strong gale-force winds came out of nowhere; I felt myself and my buggy were getting pulled to the right-hand side of the roundabout by the strong winds, and I admit I thought we were going to get blown into the cars and be killed. Out of nowhere this elderly man wearing a trilby hat and raincoat was beside me, helping me; I felt I was floating to the other side of the crossing! When I managed to compose myself I turned round to thank him, but he had disappeared! I knew it was my angel and I still feel him around me at times when I need him. I thank him for saving our lives at a very frightening time.' – YVONNE

- assist when we are born

- escort us as we cross over to heaven

'My lovely mum-in-law was fighting cancer. She was at home in her final hours and the family were sitting by her bedside holding her hand as she slept. All of a sudden, this beam of gold light touched her hip. As it did so she jolted and very shortly after she passed over, with us all by her bedside.' – CHELLE

- alert friends into action

- warn us when we are in potential danger

- help heal us when we are sick (and sit by the bedside)

'When I was little I had tonsillitis. I was seriously ill at the time because I was allergic to the medicine. The doctor was unaware and he kept giving me more of the medication because I didn't seem to improve.

'Then one day I remember quite clearly waking up in the night. There at the foot of my bed was my guardian angel. I am sure he knew what was going on and was keeping an eye on me.' – TRACEY

LEARNING ABOUT YOUR GUARDIAN ANGEL

Why not give your guardian angel a name if you haven't been given one already? Your angel will be delighted. Often we'll get a sense of whether they 'feel' masculine or feminine. You can pick a traditional angel name or create something magical of your own. Alternatively you can do a guided meditation and ask your angel for a name. I'll tell you how to do this later in the chapter.

'I had been attending a psychic development class for a while and had been asking for my guide to make contact with me. One night I'd fallen asleep and suddenly a voice yelled, "I'M ANNIE FROM THE LIGHT" and there was blinding light in my room. I've never been so startled in all my life!' – LISA

You can also communicate with your angel by writing in a journal. Let's have a look at that.

COMMUNICATING WITH YOUR GUARDIAN ANGEL

Answering Questions

Try and set aside a little time each week or each day when you can communicate with your guardian angel. Sit quietly with a notebook and write down your questions to your angel. Ask yourself, 'If I knew the answers, what would I write?' and just let the answers flow from your pen. You can do this on the computer if you prefer and type your answers out.

If you want you can create a little ritual out of it. Light some candles before you start, play some angelic-type music, place an angel statue on the table in front of you and maybe burn some incense or infuse some aromatherapy oils in an oil burner. You decide on the fragrances that are appropriate for you. Whatever makes you feel the most relaxed.

Receiving Messages

After you've practised this for a while, have a go at just free-flowing; ask your guardian angel to bring you messages of comfort and support. Just write away and see what you get. You will be aware of the messages beginning to form in your head. Your angel will probably use more 'flowery' words than you might use naturally yourself, and begin by calling you 'my beloved one...'

or saying 'my special child of the light, we are with you, you are loved…' If you have a problem beginning your meditation this way, simply write down one of these two 'starter phrases' (above) and let your message flow off your pen from then on.

Your answers might not always come to you right away. Your angels may bring you communications over several days, or drop inspirational ideas into your head all in one go. It's possible that your angel may bring you a human friend to help you through your troubles, too, or bring your attention to signs that may inspire you. Your answer may come in repeated words you hear on the television, radio or just while you're out and about. Or you might find a book falls off a shelf at your feet in a bookshop or library – take special note of the title and maybe flick through for inspiration. Better still, take the book home and read it – you'll likely find the information you have been looking for.

One woman literally had a dream in which she was given my name (she had no prior knowledge of who I was, but found my books and the answers she had been seeking were there).

Working with Meditation

You can also sit with your guardian angel in meditation each day. If you pick the same time each day or week, your angels will be waiting for you. Try and remember to keep your appointment!

Find a quiet place to sit in a comfy chair (not one that pushes back too much or you might fall asleep). Or you can sit cross-legged on the floor if you prefer. I like to have my back to the wall as it makes me feel more secure… with your eyes closed. If you are in a chair you might want to put your feet on a cushion to keep them up off the floor. I always wear socks because my feet get cold, and I have a beautiful lightweight cream throw that I place over my legs. Wear loose, warm clothing.

Time to put the dogs and cats outside, make sure the children are safe or are being looked after by someone else. Switch off your phone, light a scented candle and turn on some lovely relaxing music. Then when you're ready, we can begin our visualization. (You might want to record yourself reciting this so you can just close your eyes and relax fully.)

MEETING YOUR GUARDIAN ANGEL MEDITATION

You are strolling along a sea shore. The sound of the waves going in and out is making you more and more relaxed. The sun is shining and there is no one else around. You have the whole beach all to yourself. You hear birds singing above you and you continue to stroll, all the while listening to the waves… in and out… in and out.

Then in the distance you see a bright ball of light. The light moves towards you and you can feel that the energy inside is peaceful and calm. The energy is safe and you feel protected and comfortable as the light moves towards you, and as it does so the light grows ever bigger. Inside the light is your very own guardian angel, a glowing ball of unconditional love. You and your angel embrace. Your angel holds you in their arms and immediately you feel a charge of beautiful bright light flood through your body.

Ask Your Angel's Name

It is at this time that you can ask your guardian angel their name. Be ready for what you hear; the name might be familiar to you – in that it is a name common in your part of the world – or the name might feel more exotic to you. Your angel's name may sound like a traditional angel name that you have heard of. Maybe your angel will ask you to give them a name… because their 'name' doesn't translate into a human sound. Just accept what you hear, or choose a name, and know you will remember it so that you can write it down after the meditation.

Ask for a Message from Your Angel

It is appropriate to ask your guardian angel for a special message. Your angel will be delighted at the opportunity of meeting with you face to face. Know that your angel messages will always be loving; they are never judgemental and always supportive of your choices. Your angel will never tell you what to do, but might offer suggestions or ideas for your journey forward.

Ask Your Angel a Question

You can ask your guardian angel any questions you might have. If you are looking for help with any of your life problems, it's likely that your angel can do something to help. You may get your answer during the meditation, or a sign will appear in the days or weeks following your meditation to indicate that your angel has heard your request and is ready with some sort of assistance.

Ask for Healing

It may be the right time to ask for some healing from your guardian angel during your meditation. Make sure you are really relaxed and, once you have asked for help, just sit quietly while your angel works on your energy field (aura). It's likely that your angel may be able to make a few simple adjustments for you. Sometimes you may even feel this happening; if so you will notice a sort of tingling or fluttering in your body, or notice the gentle warmth of the healing light upon your body.

Ask for Support for Others

At any time you may ask your guardian angel to watch over others; your angel will connect with other people's angels to do this for you. You will not *interfere with that person's free will – the angels will help in whatever way they are permitted to do so. Imagine (visualize) the angel sitting above the car while your loved one drives, or flying alongside the plane your loved one is on, etc.!*

Ask for Comfort

If you're feeling lonely or sad, your meditation is the perfect time to ask for loving support from both your angels and human friends. Your angels may give you a hug right there and then (and you will feel this) or may arrange for relatives or friends (even new friends) to come into your life.

When you've finished your meditation you can sit quietly for a moment and just recall all the things you've discussed or experienced. Then when you are ready, open your eyes and slowly bring your consciousness back into the room. Take your time, maybe give your arms and legs a little shake, blow out the candle if you lit one. If you wish, make a few notes on your experience. What was your angel's name? Did you ask for a message? Did you ask questions? Write down both the questions and the answers. Record any symbols you received, colours you saw or images you want to remember – just do a simple sketch. Always remember to thank your angels for any help they bring you.

If you really felt as if you didn't meet your angel or you are worried that you 'made up' the encounter, don't worry. Angels are created during our visualizations. The experiences are real. Practise as much as you can and your experiences will become more real, more vivid as you find yourself more able to relax.

In time your meditations may take on a life of their own, as many people have encounters with higher-level guides, and even have mystical occurrences such as out-of-body experiences. Don't panic, though, these things usually only happen to those people who practise a lot! The more experienced you are, the more magical encounters with your angel you'll have.

MEDITATION SECRETS

If you are new to meditating, then you'll find the use of relaxation music helpful to quiet your body and mind. Even better, if you are a real beginner then I recommend a guided meditation (I have developed several myself) in which a voice guides you through a series of mind-actions to help you visualize an end goal (i.e. 'Meet your guardian angel'). You can buy these on CD.

As you become more experienced at meditation, the things that worked for you at first may no longer apply. Here are some of the things that helped me:

- Work in complete silence. Actually it's hard to create complete silence because there is usually a clock ticking somewhere, a pet making background noise, neighbours, children playing in the street or vehicles passing by outside. At least without music I find it easier to concentrate and completely still my mind.

- Don't move! Seriously, the minute you close your eyes you'll want to scratch, rub, cough, swallow – anything to distract you from your end goal. If you can keep completely still you'll more quickly move into the next level of consciousness; you'll actually feel the shift if you're lucky.

- Make sure your body is neither too hot nor too cold. If you get too hot you'll probably just fall asleep, which does kind of defeat the object of the exercise.

- Sit, don't lie down. Again, as above, if you lie down or your position is too 'laid back', you'll just fall asleep. You need to be fairly upright but comfortable enough so that your head doesn't drop to one side as you start to relax.

- I find the best time to meditate is during the day, not too soon after a meal and not too long until the next one – a hungry tummy is yet another distraction. Too close to bedtime at either end of the day and you'll just fall asleep again.

- Build up your meditation time a bit at a time. For beginners, 10–20 minutes is plenty. With practice there is no reason why you can't do an hour or so at a time. If you get the house to yourself occasionally, take the opportunity of meditating for longer: several hours or more.

- Deep meditation states (the place your mind will go after longer lengths of time) will inevitably lead to more unusual types of 'psychic' experiences. If you want to meet with your guides and angels, then this is where you'll want to be.

- Things to watch out for include a vibrational feeling that occurs before the consciousness separates from the physical body and generates an out-of-body experience (OBE). There is not enough room to explore this experience fully in this book (I have written about some of my experiences in *An Angel Saved My Life*). An OBE is where the spirit part of you separates from your physical body. You are connected together by a silver cord (which you may not see) so you cannot get lost if you explore other realms.

- During the simple OBE you may find you're just floating around your home. This in itself is bizarre, but as long as you keep calm you can enjoy the experience for longer. Enjoy experiencing the flying sensation; the more you practise this type of deep meditation, the more these trips will occur.

- You may see beings/spirits or angels, but at all times you must remember that you are in charge of the meditation session. You can open your eyes to bring yourself back into the room and end your mystical experience. If you feel afraid you can also ask for your guardian angel to make themselves visible for protection. The Archangel Michael, with his flaming sword of protection, can also be called in to help banish any unwanted beings you see or sense during your meditation session! Try not to worry, though, as these things usually happen only with prolonged and regular meditation sessions.

- Do investigate this type of phenomenon more if you get to the stage where you are meditating more than 20 minutes a day! Enjoy!

WORKING WITH ANGEL CARDS

Angel cards are sold in packs of around 42–48 individual cards, usually beautifully illustrated and with wonderful angelic-inspired affirmations. Each pack is usually accompanied by a book of instructions (or ideas) on how to use the pack. I have designed and created my own beautiful Angel Secrets Cards (details at the back of the book) but many other angel teachers have styled their own so there are plenty to choose from. Many bookstores sell these, as well as new age stores and gift shops. You can also buy them online.

Angel cards are safe and easy to use, and a fantastic way of making angel contact. You can select one or two cards from the pack after shuffling them, or ask a question of your angels first of all before you pick your card. In time you will find your own way of using an angel pack and maybe create your own special rituals using candles, crystals and oils. Make angel cards something you use on a regular basis to tune in to your angelic communication more. Place a pack of angel cards in an open dish on a coffee table in your living room, or place a pack on a desk or by your bed and select one or two for guidance every day.

RANKS OF ANGELS/ANGELIC HIERARCHY

Where do the angels come from? We already know that angels are created by God, but each angel has its own specific role and duties. During the 4th or 5th century, Pseudo-Dionysius the Areopagite (also known as St Denis) created a list of angels and their heavenly positions or 'orders' in his book *De Coelesti Hierarchia* (*The Celestial Hierarchy*). In the Middle Ages others brought forward their own suggestions, often working from this original list or expanding it using their own ideas.

Thomas Aquinas (1225–1274) used the New Testament as one of his references to create his list: an angelic triad with each level having three choirs (or orders) of angels. These spheres or hierarchies show the different levels of angels with the seraphim, cherubim and thrones being closest to God, and the angels (guardian angels), archangels and principalities (or princes) being closest to humankind.

First Sphere

1.1   Seraphim
1.2   Cherubim
1.3   Thrones

Second Sphere

2.1   Dominions
2.2   Virtues
2.3   Powers or Authorities

Third Sphere

3.1   Principalities or Rulers
3.2   Archangels
3.3   Angels

The higher-ranking angels are associated with being at God's right hand. They work in praising God, and are the singing angels. The angels (and sometimes archangels) are mostly connected to Earth, and these are the angels you'll be most connected to.

The Archangels

I'm sure you will be familiar with the names of the Archangels Michael and Gabriel, even if you don't know what they do. Michael and Gabriel are the only two angels mentioned by name in the New Testament, and along with Raphael are the ones we remember the most. The name 'archangel' comes from the Greek word *archangĕlos* and means chief angel, an angel of high rank.

Within the Roman Catholic Church the archangels Michael, Gabriel and Raphael are celebrated with a special feast day called Michaelmas or the Feast of St Michael and All Angels (29 September); the Greek Orthodox honour the archangels with a special day, too (8 November).

Surprisingly, archangels are only mentioned twice in the New Testament; Michael is referenced in Jude 1:9 and 1 Thessalonians 4:16, where the 'voice of an archangel' will be heard at the return of Christ.

Seven archangels are usually listed in angel books (although I have found references to many others); these seven traditional angels are first found in the Book of Enoch, which lists Michael, Gabriel, Raphael, Uriel, Raguel, Remiel and Saraqael. Others in common use today include Ariel (sometimes confused with Uriel), Azrael, Chamuel, Haniel, Jeremiel (maybe a variation on Remiel), Jophiel, Metatron, Raziel, Sandalphon and Zadkiel. I feel sure these may be the angels that work closely with the Earth realm, which means other planets, etc. have their own archangels, too. No doubt this is just the 'tip of the iceberg'!

If you wish to ask the archangels to work with you alongside your own guardian angels, then it's OK to do so. Each of the archangels has specific tasks and roles – specialities if you like. The following table will help you to decide which archangel to call upon.

Archangel Name	Meaning of the Name	Role/Specialisms
Ariel	Lion of God	Nature, birds, animals, fish, fairy and nature kingdoms
Azrael	Whom God Helps	Angel of fishermen, spiritual blockages, assists souls on their journey to heaven
Chamuel	He Who Sees God	Protection and guardianship of the Earth, soulmates
Gabriel	God Is My Strength	Messenger angel, communication
Haniel	Glory of God	Women's energies, the moon, psychic and mystical connections, magic
Jophiel	Beauty of God	Creative and manifesting angel, spiritual growth
Metatron	Angel of the Presence	Record-keeper, relationships, children, reading, recording of information
Michael	He Who Is Like God	Protection, money, the judger of souls... and all-round slayer of dragons!
Raphael	God Heals	Anything to do with health and healing, also the patron of travellers
Sandalphon	Prince of Prayers	Carries messages and prayers to heaven, watches over unborn children
Uriel	Light or Fire of God	Earth healing and manifestation

'I ask Archangel Michael to watch over my house especially when I'm out or away from home... and then I say, "only if he's not too busy elsewhere!"' – **KIRSTIE**

SPIRIT GUIDES

As well as having the support of the angels and archangels, we also have the loving guidance of spirit guides. A spirit guide is a disincarnate spirit (a soul without body), usually invisible, whose primary role is to keep us to our Earth life contract. Before birth we agree or request that we have the opportunity of learning specific lessons for the soul. Earth is a wonderful school of learning! Your spirit guide carries your 'earthly map and guide book' for you, ensuring that you are in the right place at the right time and meet the correct people that you are meant to meet upon your life's journey.

Like your guardian angel, your spirit guide may indicate a name to you – or you can ask for one to be given. If no name comes forward for you after a few days or so, then feel free to create one!

Listen for the messages of your guide. At first your angels, guides and deceased loved ones will all 'feel' the same to you, but in time you will learn to recognize the difference. Your guide may place a hand on your shoulder when you sense them close by, or maybe you'll get a type of tingling in your body. Maybe your angel brings a sort of excitement or feeling of peace, and loved ones bring a familiar scent or feeling… maybe you even visualize them in your head at the moment of contact. Make notes of each experience so that you learn the difference between contacts.

ANGEL ALTARS AND RITUALS

Although we don't need items decorated with angels in our homes, I love them. They always lift my spirits. Angels don't need to be worshipped or prayed to, but it's wonderful to include them in your angel rituals. A ritual is any sort of ceremony that includes a regular and recognized repetitive action. Lighting candles, saying magical words, using crystals, oils or herbs are all ways of creating a ritual.

Although you might prefer to have specific ways of communicating with your guardian angel, to be honest in the end it just comes down to personal preference: what makes you feel good, and what seems to work for you.

An angel altar is really just a display of objects you have collected together for a specific purpose. Your angel 'altar' is just an arrangement of objects that have particular meanings for you and your angels – shells from the beach, angel figurines, flowers, etc. Why not have a go at creating your own displays? I have them all over the house, but my favourite is in my study. It's an ever-changing arrangement of feathers, sparkly glasses (which I have hand-painted) in which I keep incense, candles and so on, angel figurines, smudge sticks (to cleanse the space in which I work), crystals and other magical items.

Candles

Candles are lit as a way of signifying 'bringing in the light', and of course angels are beings of light, so this is an important part of any angel ritual. Light the candle at the beginning of the session and then blow it out at the end as a ritualistic way of signifying the end of your ritual or working session.

Different coloured candles also have different meanings so you can create displays for a specific purpose, changing them each week if you want. Here are some candle colours and their traditional associations.

Colours	Traditional Associations
Gold	Protection, developing yourself spiritually, rituals relating to children
Silver	Rituals relating to female issues (especially health), associated with the moon
Yellow	Used for creative work and attraction
Red	Passion, of course, but also willpower and strength
Blue	Dreams, meditation and truth
Green	Balance, fertility, employment and growth
Black	Protection, removing all negativity
White	White is for peace, calm and quiet but can be used in rituals to replace any other colour candle
Purple	Developing psychic ability, anything magical
Pink	Rituals relating to love

Crystals

Lots of crystals are appropriate for working alongside your guardian angels, but some have traditional meanings that make them more useful. I use large clear quartz crystal clusters in my workshops, meditations and the rituals I do at home. Those clear points seem to positively sing with joy when I hold them. They are expensive but I've found them a worthwhile investment. Keep them clean and dust-free for best effect. Place on a rainbow lightbox for best effect, or stand them next to a candle so the colours twinkle! Try also the soft pink crystal rose quartz and magical amethyst. These are really easy to buy.

Angel Figurines

I have a vast selection of angel figurines. They've come from all over the place, and many are gifts. I especially love the plain creamy-white ones or those sprayed gold. Some of mine have even come from charity sales and cost very little indeed. Of course I also have some larger figurines that stand outside my house and in more prominent positions around my home. These often go on outings to my workshops and book-signings! Add one or two figurines to your displays.

Angel-decorated Objects

Over the years I've collected all sorts of angel memorabilia, and my displays usually incorporate a few things including angel cards (I have a vast collection), angel-wings trinket boxes (great to hold candles and smaller packs of angel cards and crystals), cherub figures which can sit on the sides of bowls, stand in plant pots or hug candles, an angel-decorated vase and an angel-decorated oil burner! Search out your own fun items and your collection can grow over the years, maybe with gifts from others – ask for them as birthday and Christmas presents.

Angel Books

The covers of some of my angel books are so pretty I often make them part of my display. You can stack your angel books in a pile on your altar or pick up a plate-stand to make them stand up! Place them at the back of your display and then put smaller items along the front.

Sparkly Shawls, Lacy Tablecloths

I have quite a selection and sometimes use scarves as tablecloths. Look out for lengths of glittery dress fabric at your local fabric shop, too. They can turn a cheap chipboard table into a rich-looking magical display. This is also the perfect time to use Grandma's hand-crocheted lace tablecloth. What better way of incorporating her energy into your arrangement?

Natural Objects

No display is complete without making use of natural objects. Fresh flowers (or a flowering plant) are really important to bring life and energy to your collection. You can also bring in shells, driftwood (lovely wrapped in coloured 'fairy-lights'), pretty pebbles and beautiful seed-heads. Even a vase of fresh leaves (decorated with angels, of course) is wonderful. Consider adding some pots of fresh-growing herbs, too.

Homemade Items

The best objects are often those you have made yourself. You don't have to spend lots of money (or even any money at all). Wildflowers in jam jars, pebbles you've painted or decorated yourself, and angel artwork in a recycled frame can look just as wonderful. You can pick up 'tumbled' crystals (smooth crystals) from gift shops for under a pound, and you probably have candles of some sort at home already. Use what you already have and then search at yard sales, boot sales and charity shops to build your collection over time.

USING YOUR ANGEL ALTAR

You can use your angel altar for many things, but mine is mainly just to lift my spirits each time I pass by. I also place candles on my display and light them before and after I meditate. You can sit next to your display to read your angel books, use your angel cards or write in your journal.

You can create special displays for different reasons. Use the candle colours suggested to enhance your intent. Here are a few suggestions for different types of angel altars:

- Change the display to match each season of the year: 'theme' them for spring, summer, autumn and winter, bringing different types of flowers and different coloured cloths and accessories.

- Choose a colour theme: red one week, then green the week after and blue the week after that!

- Birthday and celebration displays: add celebration-themed items, awards or photographs of events, then add your angel-inspired objects.

- Memorial displays: add a photograph of a lost loved one, include a personal item on the display and keep a white candle burning. (Do not leave the candle unattended.)

- Manifestation display: gather objects together to represent something you want to bring into your life – a baby, a new job, a new relationship or a new house, for example!

Say a few words or write a few words on a piece of paper or card and add it to the display using a photo frame or clip. You can also roll your paper up like a scroll – secure it with an elastic band, ribbon or piece of garden twine. Remember to thank the angels for your request or, alternatively, ask the angels to celebrate the future event with you. Write your own messages. Here are a couple of examples:

'Thank you, angels, for bringing a new baby into my life.'

'I invite my angels to help celebrate the new spring.'

Remember to light your candle before you say your special words; you can then sit quietly while you contemplate your request, visualizing the outcome. Or you can meditate on the whole thing – try and spend at least 15 minutes a day, several days in a row if you can. Make the object of your desire stronger by focusing your intent. Blow out the candle after you finish.

Keep objects fresh and clean. Regularly change the water on your flowers, remove dead flowers, wash crystals – they sparkle better when they are clean. Make sure everything is dust-free. When you look at your display and it no longer excites you, then you know it's time to take everything off and start again. Most of all, have fun – each display will reflect the personality of the person who created it!

Loved Ones as Angels

'Friends are kisses blown to us by angels.'
AUTHOR UNKNOWN

Many years ago when I first began collecting angel
stories, I realized that what many called 'a story of
angel intervention' was actually a visit from a deceased
loved one. I realized quite quickly that our loved ones
on the other side long to reach out and help us, in
much the same way that our angels do from heaven.
Their care and interest in our lives reach out in the
same way as if they had lived on.

Our deceased loved ones are still concerned about
our lives, our interests, our activities, and they want
to follow along with our life stories. They pay specific
attention to our achievements: passing an important
exam, getting through a driving test, being there as
we receive our awards and certificates. Even though we
can't see them, it doesn't mean they aren't aware of our

successes. Your loved ones are proud of you and cheer you on from heaven.

I've received many stories over the years of how deceased loved ones were seen to be peering over the cot of newborn babies, sitting at the bedside while living relatives were in hospital or calling out from the backseat of the car to warn of dangers on the road ahead.

Whether they are meant to 'interfere' in our lives is a whole other matter – they seem not to be bound by the same 'non-interference' rules as our angels and guides. I think it fair to say that if your late granny was the type to give her full and frank opinion on your unruly boyfriends when she was alive, then she'll probably do the same now she's dead. Just because she is heaven-side doesn't mean she has suddenly turned into a saint! Our loved ones on the other side are able to glimpse a little more information than we are aware of on this side, though… taking all that into consideration, we still have to make up our own minds about whether to go on that second date or not – whatever Gran thinks!

SAVING LIVES

One of the ways that our loved ones in heaven seem best able to help is in saving lives, sometimes even literally pulling us out of danger. I wonder if we are more likely to tune in to the voice of someone we've known and loved. Although the voice comes out of the blue, people certainly sit up and pay attention if their late granddad is yelling 'STOP!' at the top of his voice.

'My two grandmothers, one I've never known, are always with me in case of emergency. I cried for their help when I had to save my mum's life during a crisis one day. I shouted their names and yelled for them to assist me. Suddenly I became very calm and dialled for an ambulance and began life-saving techniques on her body. After 15 minutes the ambulance crew arrived and told me that because of my "cool" reaction, I'd saved my mum's life! Thank you, my lovely grannies.' – **PAMELA**

THE DREAM VISITATION

The other thing that I have discovered is that the phenomenon of afterlife contact is becoming more and more common. When I first started my research (a long time ago!), these types of paranormal experiences were rarer. These days it is very common for at least one family member to have had some sort of afterlife contact.

This is where you realize that 'something' truly is going on; our world is changing and we with it. As we become more evolved as souls in a human body, mystical experiences grow more and more to become part of our normal lives. Everyone who has had that one-off moment of bizarreness, that odd occasion when something didn't fit normal reality, will know that life is not the same as it was. It's only when presented with a long list of things that might trigger your memory that you might be reminded of something strange in your own life. Have any of the following happened to you?

- You knew who was on the phone or at the door even before you could see or hear the person.

- You feel that someone is staring at you and you turn round and realize you are correct.

- You get the urge to drive a different way to work, or leave home at a later time for no obvious reason, then discover you missed a road traffic accident that would have placed you at the scene had you left at your usual time.

- You get the urge to contact an old friend and at the same time discover they are trying to contact you.

- You think of someone you haven't seen in years and then bump into them.

- You remember an old friend or think of a distant family member you haven't spoken to in years and discover they've just passed away.

- You idly think about something or mull over a question and someone else in the room answers your unspoken question or begins randomly talking about the same thing (or the other way round).

- You dream of deceased loved ones but know even during the experience they are really dead.

- You call in unexpectedly at a friend's house and discover they needed urgent help.

- You need some strange or unusual thing and someone offers you the exact thing you've been looking for.

- You ask for a sign that you are not alone and find white feathers or other signs.

- You know what someone is thinking before they say it.

- You have moments where reality is not quite what it should be.

- You get lots of déjà vu moments.

- You just know when something is going to happen.

- You get a gut feeling that someone you care about is in trouble… and they are.

- You have 'memories' of a time when you could fly or do other unusual things, or you just feel you are not from here!

- You have memories of other lifetimes or other places… or planets with different types of beings! (Yes, honestly!)

MEDITATE MORE

Try and meditate every day if you can – just 10 or 15 minutes a day is great (more at the weekend or when you have more time). Try and meditate at the same time each day if you can – this is the ideal situation, but if you can't make this sort of schedule work for you, at least have a go several times a week. There are lots of books and websites that show you how to do this in more detail so I won't go into it here.

CONTEMPLATION

Try and spend more time in contemplation, too. By this I mean sit and write in a journal, go for a walk or sit looking out over a sea, river or lake whenever you can. Maybe you can create a special place at home to do this? You can place a log or bench in the corner of your garden to sit on and surround it with scented plants, beautiful figurines (angels maybe), or decorate it with tea-lights in jars or outdoor 'fairy lights'.

You can do this even in a very small yard or perhaps place a seat against the wall at the back of your property and surround it with a few pots; anywhere that's safe to sit with your eyes closed. Maybe you have only a balcony? This will work just as well or, failing that, place some scented flowers or herbs in a pot on your windowsill, hang up some angel pictures, light some incense or burn some aromatherapy oils in a special burner – light a candle and there you go, instant relaxation! Play some gentle and relaxing music in the background. Go and make your angel contemplation or meditation space today. If you have a little more room maybe you can create several special areas. You are limited only by your imagination. This would be the ideal space to read your angel books or use your angel affirmation cards.

MANIPULATING THE ENERGY AROUND US

It's amazing how 'they' can interact with us on this side of life. Our spirit friends are so active! This next story just blew me away. What do you think?

'My godson Sidney died unexpectedly and tragically of Sudden Infant Death Syndrome. Two months after my godson passed away I was making something to put on his grave. It was a box of wood and straw, 60 x 40cm, with little handles. Inside I made a representation of the world with little children: kids from America, China, Europe, etc. After a week the box was finished. I used wood, straw, paper, everything that burns really well. I was really proud of my work and it was perfect to put on a little child's grave.

'On the last evening I put a varnish on it, so it could stand in the rain. I made it completely waterproof. As I was spraying, I didn't pay attention to one of my candles, which stood on the same table, only a metre away. Of course the gas from the can set the whole thing on fire, and in just a second the whole box was alight. Can you imagine? The big flame was like a blowtorch and went right up to my ceiling; I saw the flames licking against the old dry wood ceiling!

'The flames were twice as big as the box itself and as I screamed the dogs ran away in fear. All I could think to do was to take hold of one of the handles and throw the whole thing on the floor. We'd just bought the house, and everything was old and so dry so I quickly took hold of the other handle and dragged it (while still screaming) into the kitchen. The door was open so I continued dragging it until it was safely outside!

'The flames now came up my hands and arm and I was terrified. When the fire department came, the fire was almost out. Everybody was looking in the sitting room but there was NO sign of a fire! The old wooden ceiling was clean… the carpet (which was so old) had no burn marks. On my table lay a tablecloth… it looked brand new! Nobody could explain it. I had no wounds on my hands or arm.

'A few days later, I stood in front the grave and asked Sidney if he had something to do with it. It was a cloudy but bright day and, just as I asked, little raindrops fell on me. I began to laugh and asked, "Sidney, are you doing this?" and it immediately stopped raining again.' – PAMELA

Could Sidney have put out the fire in the house? Maybe he had a little help! I know for sure that Sidney will have realized that the special creation that Pamela had taken such care of had been crafted in his honour. I have no doubt that he had more than a little involvement in Pamela's welfare. Thank goodness she was OK. Imagine what a tragedy this could have turned out to be.

This next experience is fabulous, too. It shows that our loved ones (as usual) are not against a little humour. Many years ago there was a TV programme many of you will remember called *This Is Your Life,* in which celebrities were brought back into contact with old friends, family and famous work colleagues they'd encountered over the years. Is this next dream visitation, a reference to this old show? Take a look for yourself!

'I had a dream where I was at the top of the stairs at my grandma's old house (she had passed away) and this man jumped out of the bedroom and said "This is your life", and proceeded to introduce me to all my relatives who had passed over… it was so exciting. I could hear them walking up the stairs and then hugging them all and saying "You are just as I imagined you would look" (as some had passed over before I even knew them)… I remember it so well as it was not like a dream at all!' – **Becky**

One of the signs we've talked about in the 'Signs from Above' chapter is our loved ones' ability to flicker lights on and off from the other side. But what if they *are* the light? Light features in a lot of the stories my readers share with me. This was a particularly magical experience:

'My grandfather passed away 16 years ago on 10 January. On 31 January he came to visit me (it was also his birthday). As he appeared, my bedroom was lit up with green lights. I could see my grandpa float down and he lay beside me. I've always believed the other green lights flying around my room were both our guardian angels.' – **Olivia**

Stella comes from the USA. She is a friend of mine on Facebook and used to have a website describing many of the experiences she's had over the years. She sent me the link to her site and gave me permission to use these experiences here.

'I was so excited about the many different things that happened before and after my dad's death that I just had to share these with my friends and neighbors on both sides of my house. They were not as excited as I was. In fact, both neighbors started ignoring me for a while.

'About six months after Dad died, my one neighbor came over and said, "Stella, I want to apologize to you. When you told me things that happened after your dad died, I thought you were crazy until these things happened to me." She and her husband had planned to go to Georgia one weekend to visit his mom, but something told both of them that they needed to go and visit her parents instead. That night many strange things happened and, the next day, her dad died. They were thankful for that last night they were able to spend with him as well as the events before and after that told them that her dad is fine and in good hands.

'I was told in a dream in the middle of the night by my dad (who always called me "Stelle" with an "e" at the end instead of the "a" for "Stella") that my husband Ken would lose his job but not to worry because there was a reason for it. I woke up the next day, remembered the dream and laughed. After all, when Ken got his job he was promised he could have it as long as he wanted it. I thought the dream was my imagination until a few days later when my husband came home in the afternoon and told me he had lost his job. I thought he was joking until I saw the personal items that he had brought home and the severance check. After this I remembered the dream and realized I was being prepared for what was to come.

'A few months later my husband got a new job, and we knew we had to move. I saw a big two-story white house in a dream. In my dream I also saw a big church near the house. My husband came home from work and told me about a two-story house he had seen for sale. We looked at it and it was the same house I had seen in my dream a few days before. We got the house with no money. It became a rest home for the elderly and disabled and we became administrators of the rest home… with no previous experience. The house was paid for totally in just two years. We kept the rest home for a couple of years after that and then our neighbor, who worked for us, ended up buying the house and kept the rest home going for many more years after that.

'Ken's mom was in the nursing home. We and her other family took many pictures of her with her family in the nursing home and, when she died, we made a memorial DVD to show to people the night before her funeral.

'Ken and I tried to get as many photos together as we could, with the intention of putting the pictures and accompanying music on the DVD. We went to bed tired and when I woke up someone told me that night (probably his mom) that we needed to add some younger photographs to go with the nursing home photos. I wanted to do a better job with it, but knew when we woke up the next morning there would be no time. We had to get ready for the funeral and then had a long drive afterward. We decided to quickly add some younger photographs and leave it at that; the spacing wasn't how I'd have liked it and there was just no time to add music.

'Later when we watched the DVD, we were stunned. The younger pictures of her we had added at the beginning were spaced beautifully and you could hear music playing in the background. When we got to the older photos of her in the nursing home, these just rushed past really quickly, almost as if they didn't matter. Then near the end there were some more photos of her when she was younger, and again these were spaced right and not rushed through. We realized that we had been helped with this DVD, as there was no human way we could have done it this way in the time we had.

'We told her granddaughters, who had taken care of her the last two years of her life, that their grandma was really good with computers. They looked at me like I was crazy until we explained about the DVD. I fully believe that she helped us with her memorial DVD and did it her way!' – STELLA

LOVE FROM THE OTHER SIDE

Everyone is looking for a little love and acknowledgement; love and acknowledge someone today! When those words remain unspoken we carry regret both on this life and the next. Often our loved ones come back to say the words they couldn't say when they were on this side of life. 'I love you, I am proud of you.' Who doesn't want to hear that? Of course we all do. Take my advice… do it now!

A Guiding Hand

'By confronting us with irreducible mysteries that stretch our daily vision to include infinity, nature opens an inviting and guiding path toward a spiritual life.'

THOMAS MORE

WHO ARE YOU?

We are awakening to our true selves. Many of us have been previously incarnated on other planets and on other worlds or in different dimensions. Maybe you too are here to help the planet evolve. This hectic world of ours means that we forget our true identity. As we enter our human bodies at birth we have no idea who we really are – but this is changing.

Thousands around the world are waking up to who they really are. We are spirits having a human experience – we are so much more than just our bodies. Do not be afraid. Earth is a wonderful planet (although admittedly we humans have made many mistakes with the Earth). We've already caused so much damage to our beautiful Eden, as well as sending damaging energies out into the universe. It's time for this to change. It is changing right now, so choose to be a part of it.

Our role is to love: love the planet, love the creatures that are here and love one another. Beings from other realms are already here (many of them still not aware who they are, but awaking to this knowledge day by day). Some are here just to hold positive energies to the planet; others are here to bring light to damaged parts of the world or to change those they meet, simply by encountering them physically. Maybe, like me, you are one of these beings? What is your earthly role? How do you help others? What is your role in life in this incarnation? Keep doing what you love, because the chances are, this is where your mission lies!

WORKING WITH YOUR ANGELS AND LOVED ONES TO CHANGE YOUR VIBRATION

We are so much more than flesh and blood. Humans are spirit residing in a human body. The part that is you is your spirit or soul, not your body! In several of my books I have written about out-of-body experiences. Eventually humans will evolve to the point where we don't use our solid 'heavy' human bodies at all. Here is a story from one reader who had the opportunity of having an out-of-body experience (incidentally, I have had many of these types of experience myself).

'I was listening to a relaxation CD (harp music) while lying on my bed. I felt myself relax very deeply and get very, very heavy, my eyes closed. The next thing I was aware of was a humming or buzzing sound in my mind, a bit like the noise of an untuned radio. My body seemed to vibrate very fast. I stayed calm and went with it.

'Next I felt ever so light, and had the sensation I was floating. I could then see around me but I had not opened my eyes. I had floated upwards and turned to face my bedroom window. I was still aware of the music playing, but ever so softly as though it was far away. The next thing I recall is that I was moving out of my bedroom window and, as I did, I turned and saw myself lying on the bed, which was very strange but also felt calm and safe. I "floated" over the garden for what seemed like a second, then started to think, "I wonder if I can go see my mum and dad?" (They were on holiday at the time.) No sooner had I thought this than I was hovering over my mum and dad's campervan and could see them sitting down inside.

'Then I thought, "If this is a real out-of-body experience, all I have to do is try to wriggle my fingers and toes and I will be back in my body." Well, no sooner had I thought this than, snap! I was back in my room lying on my bed. I was kicking myself for not making the most of the experience. The whole thing was surreal, but definitely not a dream. I have had lucid dreams before and this was not

*one of them. I was as aware of everything as I am in normal
waking life, but everything felt so calm and relaxed and
almost hazy. I only had to think of something and I was
there before I had even finished the thought. I was about
26 years old at the time and regretted not exploring the
phenomenon more before coming back into my body!'*
– PETA

There are lots of things you can be working on (with
the help of your loved ones on the other side, of course)
to help raise your own vibration at this time. I've
mentioned some of these earlier in the book, but let's
have a little closer look here.

CHANGE YOUR DIET

To become lighter spiritually, look at your diet. Foods
we have been able to eat our whole lives seem to be
causing problems in our bodies now.

Best Foods

Eat: fresh foods, non-processed foods, organic produce,
salad, vegetables, fruits, seeds and nuts (if you're not
allergic, of course), oily fish, olive oil and other healthy
oils – read labels! Eat more raw vegetables. Look at
sprouting beans (alfalfa, for example – preferably sprout
your own so you know they are fresh). Drink plenty
of water.

OK/Good Foods

Dairy: if you must have milk consider skimmed, and goat's milk seems easier to digest. If you must have cheese, look for low-fat options. Eggs are OK. Frozen vegetables, canned vegetables, fruit juices, chicken. Starchy vegetables (like potatoes), rice, whole grains. Eat all of these foods in moderation/smaller portions than you have done up until now.

Worst 'Foods'

Eat fewer processed foods, less salt, sugar, artificially enhanced anything, sugary drinks and snacks, fatty foods, red meat, rich sauces, cream, caffeine, sugar substitutes, alcohol. Try to give up or cut back on cigarettes. And did you know that scientists in Boston discovered that drinking one or more sodas (regular or diet) every day doubles your risk of metabolic syndrome?

Deep down inside you know all this stuff already. The best part of looking after yourself in this way is that your skin glows, your weight stabilizes and you'll have more energy. You'll also feel more energetic and just have a better feeling of well-being. Don't change everything at once, though, cut out one thing at a time. Giving up sugar is a challenge, especially if, like me, you are addicted to chocolate. You will continue to have cravings for a while. Some people report annoying side-effects like headaches, but not everyone experiences these and in any case they pass off quite quickly. Just take your time and also take advice from your doctor or dietician.

Spend a few minutes honouring your food before you eat. It was traditional at one point to 'say grace', thanking God for the food before it was eaten. Native Americans give thanks to the animal for the clothing and food its body provides. This is a great practice and we should be working along these lines each and every time we eat something. Spend a few moments giving thanks to your food for the nourishment it provides you. Imagine the life-force energizing your body as you eat.

Water is especially important to keep you hydrated. How many times do we take a painkiller because we have a headache when a glass of water would clear the source of the problem? Dehydration causes so many issues! Make sure you keep a glass or bottle of water handy while you work, and sip gently throughout the day. Don't forget to bless the water first of all – you can also follow this little ritual: hold the flat palm of your right hand (left if you are left-handed) over the top of the water (or food). Draw a spiral over the top, first in one direction and then the other. You can imagine the spiral-drawing in your head if you wish, but by doing it physically others will see and ask you about it – spread the word!

Take time when eating your food, don't rush. Enjoy each mouthful, savour it. Don't eat foods you really don't like or really aren't enjoying – it's like adding emotional poison to your body! You deserve the best, the freshest and the healthiest foods for the preservation of your body and mind.

LOVE WHAT YOU DO... AND LIVE A LONGER AND HAPPIER LIFE

If you don't love – or at least like – the work that you do, then consider looking for more enjoyable work. If money is an issue, then consider how you can spend less money each month. Do you really need all the latest electronic equipment, fancy holidays, two family cars, etc.? Could you move out of the city and into a cheaper area in the country? Could you rent out a spare room to save or make money? Remember also that if you unplug everything at the sockets when not in use you save on electricity.

We become stuck in a rut of self-made hardship because of habits we create for ourselves. Sit down with a friend for an objective view of how you could realistically change your lifestyle. The aim is to have less stress in your life and create more time and money to do the things that you love. Can you retrain for work that would bring you pleasure? Ask yourself, what would I be doing if I could do anything right now? What would I be doing for me, for fun? Use this as a clue to looking at new career opportunities.

Often when we move into work we love, we find our income goes up – but it doesn't have to. Look at ways you can change your life for the better – ask your angels and deceased loved ones to support you and help bring opportunities into your life for self-fulfilment. Live a more positive life if you can – try and let go of negative thoughts and attitudes for a happier life. Often the things that we worry about the most aren't important at all. Living with less stress can even lengthen your life.

Leslie Martin PhD, co-author of the book *The Longevity Project: Surprising Discoveries for Health and Long Life from the Landmark Eight Decade Study*, says 'What we actually found [during the project] was that the conscientious individuals, because they were on top of things and they were organized and responsible, they had a lot of opportunities that came their way and so they really often lived quite exciting and enjoyable lives.' And of contented people she said, '[They] have better health behaviours… they tended to gravitate into more stable jobs, into stable marriages, and so on.'

Just one more thing to bear in mind: Science Daily released an article in March 2011 that stated, 'A review of more than 160 studies of human and animal subjects has found "clear and compelling evidence" that, all else being equal, happy people tend to live longer and experience better health than their unhappy peers.'

LISTEN TO YOUR ANGELS

Because of the other changes to the planet, we are being permitted more interaction with our loved ones in other dimensions – this is no new age make-believe, this is real. You may even have experienced contact yourself, either consciously or semi-consciously. As you read about the phenomena you are becoming more aware and less frightened. If you are less scared, you are more likely to experience the wonders of contact from heaven yourself. Knowledge literally is power.

Sometimes these beings give us little tips about our health, as well as warnings. Shelly's angel gave her a full diagnosis!

'I was being investigated for cancer/leukaemia… my guide Argus told me that I had fibromyalgia, as I got stroppy with spirit and told them that if they thought they were going to take me then they had a fight on their hands. I have been diagnosed with fibromyalgia, just as my fantastic guide said.' – SHELLY

I once woke up to a voice that told me, 'Eat pomegranates.' Was this a message from beyond? There certainly wasn't anyone else in the house at the time. Sadly I can't stand this fruit, but I did try the juice, which was OK. I looked up the properties of the fruit on the Internet and was amazed to discover, 'The pomegranate is regarded as a type of food medicine.' The tree roots, the bark, the leaves, flowers, rind and seeds have featured in medicines for thousands of years! In ancient India it was described as a light food and a tonic for the heart! I wish I loved it! In biblical times pomegranate was considered a gift from the gods. It's a rich source of vitamins A, C and E, all three key antioxidants that help prevent heart disease and cancers. I did increase my vitamins in these particular areas at least.

Have you ever been given dietary advice from a spirit or angel?

'I wondered why I wasn't feeling too well, and then my guardian angel told me to drink more water. They also suggested I add lemon juice to salad. I make massage oils and I was drawn to lemon in this, too; when I read up on it, I was amazed that it had all the things I was lacking in.

'Since taking notice of my angels, I feel so lovely now. We really must take note of this amazing advice from above, or should I say from "around", as I believe angels are around us all the time, guiding us on our path.' – AMANDA

Here is another example, this time from a Facebook friend, Karen. The angels are busy with dietary advice, it seems.

'Just recently John (my guide) advised me to eat cherries, and I can't seem to go shopping without buying some. I have never really been that keen, but for some reason I'm finding them delicious and can't get enough of them. Normally I

*would go for strawberries or bananas if I was to have fruit.
I have arthritis developing in my knees and hands, and it's
been in my neck and spine for a while. A couple of weeks ago,
after he started me on cherries, I found out they are good for
arthritis!'* – **KAREN**

THE FUTURE OF THE PLANET

Many beings, including our loved ones, are visiting us
while we sleep. Sometimes you'll recall some of these
experiences, but other times you'll remember very little.
The information they are bringing is important but not
necessary for us to remember at this time. Here's an
example of this phenomenon in action.

*'Last Friday my nan visited me in a dream. It's frustrating
because I couldn't remember the message when I woke up.
Then last night when my daughter and I got home we could
both smell my nan's perfume, which was comforting but
I feel like she's trying to send me a message and I'm not
picking it up.'* – **HANNAH**

Some of the information we are given comes as symbols
(geometric shapes), each of which contains a whole
stack of information. In the future as the planet changes
this information will come forward and we'll wonder
how we know the things we know. The information
was given to us while we slept… we'll recall it at the
appropriate time.

We are so much more than we imagine. Our world can't be explained easily by science, but that's no one's fault – there is just way more than science can even begin to explore at this time, though it has made a start. Don't imagine that just because science can't currently explain something, this means it isn't true. It's not so long since we thought the Earth was flat, but you know what? It never was! Keep an open mind about all things. Be ready for changes. It's just a matter of time before the announcement that yes, of course there are beings on other worlds. We are not alone! There really is something out there… and there always was.

Here is an important story that illustrates the type of communication that a few of my readers are starting to receive. These are awakening dreams where we are being reminded of our life purpose (all assuming our free will, of course!).

'I was asleep in bed and I suddenly found myself falling. My guardian angel picked me up in his arms. I was nervous about looking at him but he asked me if I was ready to see him so I told him yes. He then put me down and I saw he had the most beautiful blue eyes and black curly hair. He told me his name was Egwelio.

'My angel took my hand and told me he wanted to show me something. We sort of whooshed along the ground, and then I was in front of a large building. It looked like a theatre, or the Royal Horticultural Halls in London, where the Mind Body Spirit exhibitions are held.

'He then pointed upwards and my name was up there on the boards. He said I had something very important to do and I would be very successful and well respected if I followed my guidance.

'This time is sort of coming closer now, as I've since had other messages that I will bring a new healing system to the planet for the new energies that are coming in. They'll recalibrate people's energy fields and change and reactivate their DNA strands.' – LYNN

What an amazing experience! I feel lucky in that I have been aware of my 'life mission' for a while now. Reminding people of the angels was just the beginning, though, as my future holds teaching of more complicated concepts – but it's going to be a fun ride. I hope you'll join me!

We're also being contacted by beings from other realms and planets – some of these are actually our 'home planet'! Sounds crazy? People always think that about things they don't understand! Many from other places feel lonely – an intense loneliness that they just can't get away from. Why do we feel this way even when surrounded by family and friends? I am lucky because my soul group all came with me this time round. Just know that life is eternal – we are born, we live, we change form as we leave to be reborn into spirit again. The people we have lived with on this Earth have been with us in previous lives, and will be with us again in future lives. Energy is never lost or destroyed... but it often changes form!

HELP FROM OTHER REALMS – ANGELS IN ANOTHER FORM?

Our planet is in crisis and for thousands of years we've been watched over by beings from other realms. The question is no longer 'if' they exist but 'who are they?'! To deny the existence of other life forms is to be naïve in the extreme. According to one source, there are over 400 reputable UFO witnesses in the government, military and intelligence communities. Astronauts have reported seeing unidentified craft watching them since the very first space missions.

As far back as 2001 (9 May to be exact), more than 20 people including government representatives, military and scientific witnesses took part in an event at the National Press Club in Washington, DC, to ascertain the reality of extra-terrestrial life. It included much first-hand testimony. The proof is now overwhelming. Extra-terrestrial life is real and these beings are visiting as they always have, to watch over humankind. Are they our angels? Sort of! Part of our free will is that we have been permitted to follow our own path, make our own decisions. Here is one reader's experience.

'I was sitting on my bed, talking to my brother on my mobile phone and at the same time I was looking out of the window… as you do. I remember it was a clear day, the sky was blue and I noticed a plane flying in the sky; to the left of the plane, there it was. "Oh my God…!" I shouted down the phone. "What's that in the sky?" I paused and stared, hardly believing what I was seeing.

'My brother on the other end of the line was trying to ask me, trying to speak to me, but I was fixated on this thing in the sky; I couldn't hear him. "Oh my God… it's a UFO" I shouted. My two sons came running up the stairs and looked out of the window. It was a golden sphere, flying parallel to the plane; we watched it for a while. It took off at the speed of light, much faster than the plane… so fast that I didn't even see which direction it went.

'After that I went to church as I normally did on a Sunday. I'd stopped off at a petrol station on the way to get petrol. When I got to the till I was asked, "Do you always put that in your car?" I said, "Yes," puzzled to say the least, because it was such an odd thing to be asked. The woman behind the till, I remember, had the most piercing blue eyes, and blonde hair. She continued, "Only… we've been sent here this week to help you."

'I stood there and, as silly as it seems, I thought, "What are you, an alien or angel?" It all seemed to get very strange. The people in the town all seemed to be zoned out, like they were miles away.

'But it was at night that it got even stranger. I woke up and it was dark; I was lying in bed, but I was paralysed and I couldn't move anything except for my eyes. I had *the feeling of being "scanned" by something that I couldn't see; it felt like something was scanning my body. This happened to me quite a few times over the different nights. Was this my encounter of the third kind? Ironically, I'd had reoccurring UFO dreams as a child. Reliving these in reality as an adult, well… coincidence or not?'* – STELLA

Part 3

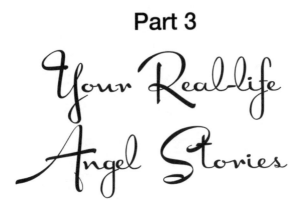

Your Real-life Angel Stories

Lisa: 'If you believe in angels then
why not unicorns or leprechauns?'
Kent Brockman: 'Oh Lisa, everyone
knows leprechauns are extinct.'

From *The Simpsons* episode 'Lisa the Skeptic' (1997)

Stories of Visitations

*'Thou hast granted me life and favour, and thy
visitation hath preserved my spirit.'*
BOOK OF JOB 10:12

A visitation, in the way I am using it here, is a real visit from a spirit or angel that occurs during our sleeping hours... although sometimes also when we are awake. For each person who experiences this there is no doubt as to its truth, as the experience leaves a lasting impression that bears little in common with dreams. Your loved one or angel appears to you while your body is asleep but your mind is awake and aware.

The same themes tend to run through this kind of real spirit contact. You can look for these in your own visitation experiences. I have covered these signs in other books, but for clarity let's go over the most common signs.

- During the experience you have awareness that you are not asleep.

- When encountering the deceased, it's common to express confusion that they are alive and to say so, using words such as 'Why are you here, aren't you dead?'

- Human friends may be accompanied by an angel or spiritual type of guide throughout the experience (who also lets them know when it's time to leave and go back to their own realm).

- The deceased will usually try to indicate to you by some measure that they are still alive, and how well and happy they are in their new heavenly home.

- They might show themselves as younger and healthier than they appeared at the point of their passing. Missing limbs are re-attached, diseased bodies are pure and free from any ailment, growths or masses.

- Messages are usually simple and speedy but normally have similar meanings:

  - I love you

  - I am safe and well

  - Stop worrying about me

  - I am healthy now (and whole)

  - I am still watching over you

  - I am proud of you

  - I am aware of what is going on in your life

  - Congratulations or well done!

I have spent some time interviewing each of the readers for the experiences in the next few chapters so that you get a little more information about what happened... behind the scenes! Let's have a look at some of these amazing experiences.

My Son Who Art in Heaven

'I'm not really sure where to start with this letter. I've never done this before! My name is Paula and just a few weeks ago three of your books showed up for sale where I work in a care home. I've always had an interest in angels, and something in my head kept telling me that I had to buy these books. I had the strongest feeling that I knew your name, but still don't know where from. Well, I bought the books and couldn't believe what I was reading; there were so many similarities with my own life. With each chapter I found myself saying, "Oh my God, that's happened to me!" I could go on for pages and pages about my experiences, but I'd just like to share a few with you that mean everything to me. Somehow I know you will appreciate them!

'My grandfather died on 31 March 1991; he was like a father to me growing up because my own father worked away from home a lot. I firmly believe he's visited me as a spirit on numerous occasions! These visits have happened in the form of "dreams".

'The first visit was about a year after he passed, I found myself in what I can only describe as a waiting room

in heaven. A woman came into the room and said to me, "He'll be ready for you in a minute, please be careful with what you say, he's in a fragile state."

'I nodded and she opened a door. At the end of a long, white room I saw my granddad sitting in a high-backed armchair in front of a television. I walked over and knelt by the side of the chair. I put my hand onto the arm of the chair and he grabbed it tightly; he seemed disturbed by something, not so much angry, more desperate. He leaned toward me and he said, "Where is your nan? Why hasn't she come to see me?"

'I didn't answer him but he continued, "What's happening to your brother, why is he hurting the family?" At the time my brother was going through drug problems, but my granddad had known nothing about this before he died.

'Granddad asked me why I hadn't brought my baby daughter in to see him too, and at this point I remember putting my arm around him to comfort him (he still had hold of my other hand) while we both cried. I reassured him that everything was OK and that he didn't have to worry any more. With that I woke up crying. My hand felt bruised for a couple of days afterwards. The dream upset me because I felt for a long time that maybe Granddad couldn't have been ready to die when he did, but after the experience I carried on with life… as you do.

'I had no more experiences until 1993. I became pregnant for a third time (I had two daughters already). Then ten weeks into the pregnancy I suffered a miscarriage. I was devastated, and even though I had two healthy, *beautiful girls my grief was enormous! Two months down the line I still felt unwell and hadn't seen a period so I was sent for a scan. Straight away they detected a heartbeat and it was very strong. Bizarrely, the scan showed that I was still pregnant. They could tell from the placenta it had been a twin pregnancy. It was like being told you're pregnant but you don't have to go through the rotten sickness stage. I have to tell you, Jacky, I was happier than I'd ever felt. They asked if I wanted to know the sex of the baby and I said no, I preferred a surprise.*

'A few nights after this I had another "dream". I was walking along a path, dressed in black and there were lots of people surrounding me, telling me how sorry they were but I didn't understand why. When I got to the end I saw the tiniest white coffin I'd ever seen, and on the top on a small white plaque was written the name "Alistair". I knew at this point I was saying goodbye to the baby I had lost, but I don't know who had named him Alistair, it's not a name I would have chosen, though I like it. Anyway, I began to get upset but when I looked up my granddad was standing in front of me looking happy, young and healthy. He threw his arms around me and said, "It's all right now, Paula, I understand what's happened and I'm happy." Then it was Granddad's time to reassure me. He said, "I don't want you to worry about your son, he'll be born healthy and well."

'Again I woke up crying, but this time I was happy. My granddad was happy and I knew I was having a son. It wasn't an easy pregnancy, I nearly lost my son twice but in the end Adam was born just two weeks early and it was the most relaxed birth I've ever known.

'I have four children now, three girls and a boy, and over the years I've noticed that in photos of my children there's always a gap as though someone is missing. Although I've suffered four miscarriages, somehow I've always known that the gap is where Alistair should be.

'Every Christmas and birthday for Adam I've thought of Alistair. Last year, out of the blue I had another dream. I was in another waiting room and a woman came into the room and said, "If you just sit there he'll be with you shortly." I sat down on a plain wooden chair and as I looked up I saw someone I initially thought was Adam standing in front of me. As I looked more closely I saw his hair was longer and curly, he was a bit thinner and his features were ever so slightly different. I walked over, put my hand on his shoulder and said "Alistair?" He nodded and a big tear rolled down his cheek, but he was smiling. We held on to each other for what felt like an eternity, I cried and said how sorry I was that I'd never got to know him, but he reassured me that I would one day. I woke that morning feeling refreshed and happy, and I thanked God for allowing me to see the son I'd grieved so hard for.

'I'm convinced my "dreams" are more than that. I remember them clearly and in such detail. I'm not sure why I have been blessed in this way, but I'm glad I have. I know my angels are around me, I'm not scared of dying and I look forward to seeing what my heaven will be like. Thank you, Jacky, for your books, I no longer feel I'm the only one who's like this!' – PAULA

Twin Sister Is Still with Us

'I come from a family of eight children (five girls and three boys) and I am the third eldest child, the eldest girl. My next two sisters (twins) were born a little more than a year after me. The younger of the twins (Vicky) died about 12 years ago when she was just 41. The whole family was devastated, as she was a much loved sister and daughter.

'The day after she died my family were all getting together to make funeral arrangements and by the end of the day it all became rather too much for my dad. He ended up in hospital because everyone thought he was having a heart attack; apparently it was the stress and anxiety, so we were relieved that he was OK. My dad has never been a big believer in angels, etc., but he told us that that night while he was lying in the hospital he opened his eyes and my sister was standing alongside him. She touched his face and told him that he shouldn't be sad because she is in a lovely place, with her mum, and everything would be OK. He has told us since that at first he thought it was just a dream, but now he isn't so sure. He felt her, saw her and knew in his heart she was with him.

'For several days after Vicky died I just couldn't sleep well because I was forever crying. Then one night while I was crying about losing her I realized that she wasn't lost because I felt her presence in the room and I heard her "shushing" me and felt her stroke my head until I went to sleep. After that I started sleeping more peacefully, knowing that she was OK.

'We all still miss her very much and my oldest daughter sees her all the time; not as a physical person but she sees the spirit of her and has conversations with her.

'Whenever we have family get-togethers we light a candle for her and we know she is there because we smell and feel her presence. I went to see a psychic woman (who was wonderful) who told me that my sister was full of life, love and wanting to find out more and more about everything. She also told me that my sister (and mum) will always be around looking after us when we need them.

'I know this to be true because when I was travelling along a road late one evening (a dark, deserted road that I had never been down before), I started to get worried that I had missed my turn-off and felt a bit of a panic coming over me. I asked Mum and Vicky to send me a sign, and what should fly straight past the windscreen of the car but a white dove (in the evening this is very unusual). I thanked them both and continued my journey in safety knowing they were watching over me.' – **PAMELA**

Nurse Button and Other Signs

'I have always been interested in the afterlife and started reading Doris Stokes' (the late psychic medium) books years ago. I used to chat with my mum, who was always ready to talk about the books I'd been reading. As the years went on my mum became ill, and on many occasions she told me she was scared… not of dying, but of what happened after. I tried to reassure her by saying my dad, who'd passed away

several years ago, would be there along with her family and
she wouldn't be left alone.

'Mum told me that if it was possible she would find a
way of letting me know she was OK, without scaring me,
and we left it at that. Mum took a turn for the worse and
we were called to the hospital. My brother, my step-father
and I rushed to her bedside. Mum slipped away soon after.
As we were gathered at the foot of her hospital bed, saying
our goodbyes, a nurse called in and asked if we were OK. I
said yes and she replied that someone had pressed the nurse
call button at the back of Mum's bed. None of us was near
it and we always wondered: was it Mum giving us a sign?
We hoped it was.

'Some time after this I was asleep one night when I had
the most vivid dream where I was in a big room with lots of
people and then my mum came walking towards me as clear
as anything and looking well. I was stunned but she came
to me and said, "You have nothing to be afraid of; when the
time comes, take my hand and come with me." I woke up
crying. Was it only a "dream"? Am I going "potty" as my
kids say when I tell them what happened? I don't think so!

'When I started going to the local Spiritualist church, I
recall on one occasion being in the house on my own. I was
cleaning and I stopped at Mum's picture at the top of the
stairs and said, "Look, Mum, I'm going to the Spiritualist
church tonight. If you can, will you try and give me a sign
you're there?" I carried on cleaning and then went back
downstairs into the kitchen. The clock fell off the wall from
above the sink, yet the nail was still in the wall and it had
never fallen before or since. Was this another sign?

'My mum never had the opportunity of travelling
abroad. She loved the sunshine and she even had a passport,
bless her, but never got to use it. I was in Turkey this month
with my husband and was chatting to some elderly people,
telling them that it was nice to see them enjoying the sun
and how my mum would have loved to be there.

'I was in bed later that day when I had a dream that
I was sitting at a table with my husband and daughter. We
were in a room when Mum came in; my husband could see
her and so could my daughter. Mum walked around the
table, stood behind me and I felt her arms wrap around me.
The love was enormous and so real! Then I awoke again
and was a little tearful.

'Later I spoke aloud saying, "Mum, if that was you,
send me a sign… a butterfly." Days passed and I kept an
eye open for the butterfly sign, but nothing happened. Then
as I was lying in the sun a woman sat down in front of me
with a butterfly tattoo on her back. It was the most beautiful
coloured butterfly. My kids laugh, but I like to think Mum
is still here with me; when it's my time she will be there
holding out her hand, just as she promised.' – LESLEY

Car Clampers

'My younger brother Clinton Berry died on 23 November
2007; he'd turned 39 on 2 November. He had suffered a
very rare and severe stroke two weeks previously.

'Clint and I had been very close as we grew up; there
was only 18 months between us. I married twice and had
four children. Clint had a string of relationships, a few

happy ones but, sadly, no children. Whenever Clint was unhappy or needing a shoulder to cry on, he came to me. He loved Mum and Dad dearly, but sometimes he didn't want them to know his worries or to cause them worry. So every so often he would arrive on my doorstep; he was always welcomed with open arms.

'Since his passing there have been a lot of little things that make us believe he is around. I had a BMW at the time, and a few times when I had my daughter Sarah in the car, the stereo would suddenly go really loud the first time, playing the song 'Valerie'. There was nothing to explain this happening – we questioned everything! "Valerie", the version sung by the late Amy Winehouse, would be playing at significant times, and other songs he liked came on at just the right times. We could be walking into shops or hear them in the car just as we were talking about him. Mum and I often find white feathers, and we have a robin that comes to say hello when I am out.

'I was in the local library a couple of weeks ago with my family. My youngest wanted to sit by the window and watch some BMX bikers through the window. I sat in a chair with her and within a couple of minutes I was drawn to look in the book section just near me, a section I never look in. I scanned the aisle and your book shone out. It was the only book I picked up, and I knew I had to read it. Two things happened in the course of my reading it. The first was me relaying a story to my mother-in-law about how I ask Clint to send me six lucky numbers. That evening I opened the book and the first thing I read was you telling me how our loved ones can't help with things like this!

'The second thing was even greater proof from Clint. I had read about dream experiences and asked him to try it. Two days later I did dream… I had been to a funeral that I had been involved in and it was a nice funeral. When I got home, though, there were lots of cars parked on my driveway so I couldn't park. There were people standing in the garden and I asked them to move their cars. They just laughed, so I replied, "I have someone I can call who will clamp your cars." I held my mobile phone in my hand and began to dial a number, but I was saying, "I can't call Clint, he's dead." Then as clear as anything I heard my brother speak to me as if he was standing facing me. He said I didn't need my phone, I could speak to him any time, he was always with me whenever I just needed to talk. I cried in my sleep and it woke me. The dream was so real, his voice as clear as anything.

'I believe this was Clint giving me a definite sign. He worked as a bailiff for many years, clamping the cars of those who didn't pay their parking fines. My mum has a video of Clint when he appeared on Watchdog talking about the car clampers, which Mum watches frequently.

'I have sent your book Angels Watching Over Me to my mum. She loved every word you wrote and I feel it has given her the comfort and reassurance she needs that her little boy is safe and he hasn't left us completely. I thank you with all my heart for that, the angels have sent you. God bless you.' – LOUISE

Happy Christmas

'Hi Jacky, I feel that I had to write to you as I have read
two of your books and am now reading a third. These
books have brought me so much comfort over these last
few months; I have suffered depression and had to receive
counselling due to the passing of both my parents, whom
I adored so much. My dad passed over in March last year
very suddenly in hospital aged 64. It tore our world apart,
and my mam was in hospital at the same time, so my two
sisters and I had to break the news to her.

'Mam could not face going back to her home, so she
came to stay with me as she did her own dialysis at home
(she had no kidneys). I was there to look after her but my
mam sank into a deep depression and, 12 weeks after my
dad had passed, I awoke to find she also had passed over in
her sleep.

'My life has changed so much, we were such a close
family and saw each other every day and spent every
Christmas together. Last Christmas Eve was our first year
without them; I could not stop crying all day and was not
looking forward to the festivities ahead. A few weeks prior
to Christmas I went to my local Spiritualist church and my
dad gave me a message to say go ahead with our plans as
normal because they would be with us.

'Christmas morning came and as always we were up
at the crack of dawn with our children; my partner Craig
and I were in the kitchen making tea when all of a sudden
a bright light shone on our portable television. I can assure
you it was not plugged in. Then we heard knocking on the

door straight after that. I went to see if anyone was there, but no one was to be seen.

'I truly believe, and my partner does, too, that my parents were letting me know that they were there to share our day with us. It brought me so much comfort and I was able to enjoy the rest of the day knowing my parents were by my side.

'I've had loads of experiences with other things… too many to mention, but I've heard my dad call out my partner's name when he got up one night to go to the toilet; my partner didn't hear it. We overslept one morning for work and my mam called out my name. I think it was because she knew that she had to get us up for work! I have always believed in the afterlife, Jacky, more so now, and I can now move forward with my life knowing that my parents are only in the next room from me; when it's my turn to unlock that door I will be united with my beautiful mam and dad and all my other loved ones.' – ANTHEA

Hello from Mrs B

'Hi Jacky, I am writing this just after returning from holiday, cases still unpacked in the hallway. My sister-in-law Judy and her husband Paul came on holiday with me and my wife Karen, Ruth, our daughter and Rebecca, our granddaughter.

'I know Judy has missed her mum deeply since her death over two years ago; we all have, she was like a mum to me from about the age of 13. I know that Judy is upset that she hadn't had a message from her mum. When we

were on holiday, Judy asked if I would like to read one of
your books. As soon as I started reading it, I was nodding
my head in agreement with all that you had written,
because most of what you say in the book has happened to
me. From a young age I have had dreams that I know are
different from normal dreams, dreams of people who have
died during the night of my dream — when the phone has
rung or I've met someone connected to them I know what
they are about to tell me. I have always kept these things to
myself apart from close family (I even tried to block
them out).

'Here are just a few. When my mum died I was in
pieces; I had nursed her with my sister Ann because she
wanted to die at home. I lifted my mum so my sister could
change her bedding; she died almost in my arms. She had
been "out of it" all day, and as I lay her back down, her
eyes opened and she stared excitedly at something in the
corner of the room. She then turned and looked at me for a
fleeting moment, then she looked back to the corner of the
room once more. It was at this point that she died.

'That night I walked my dog in the local park, and
as I looked up to the stars I said, "Please, Mum, let me
know that you are OK." Then I had this feeling of rushing
through the stars; she was on a journey and had not yet
arrived. The next morning I awoke and was putting on a
brave face for my kids. I glanced at the TV and could see a
news clip about a mass grave in Russia. As my hearing is
bad, and more so with the background noise of the kids, I
couldn't hear what they were saying, but felt sad looking at
the families crying for their lost ones at the side of the grave.

It was at this point that I moved into the kitchen to make a cup of tea, and it was then that I heard my mum's voice clearly saying, "It's Mum, and I'm OK."

'I moved quickly back into the lounge to see if the kids had changed TV channels (they hadn't). This was one of many messages that I have received from my mum; I have spoken with her in dreams, heard special songs on the radio, etc.

'Going back to Judy, I'd nicknamed her mum "Mrs B" many years ago. Not long after her death I had one of those dreams, you know, these types of dreams. In the dream I opened a door and walked down some steps that led to what looked like an empty room, apart from some old style hospital ward curtains. I looked to the bottom of the curtains and could see some legs that were covered by an old type hospital auxiliary uniform; it was a checked yellow mustard colour.

'I knew straight away that it was Mrs B, and called to her, "Mrs B!" Then the curtain opened and there was Mrs B, smiling at me. "Hi, Ant," she said. I asked her, "Are you OK?" She assured me she was, and she was smiling. "Can I touch you?" I asked, and she told me I could. I held her hands and moved closer to her, then without asking I flung my arms around her to give her a hug, and leaned forward to give her a kiss on her cheek, but she fell backwards and I fell forwards into a type of cloudy mist. I could see a small face (like these alien faces people see), but this was small. I sprang backwards and there was Mrs B again. "You're not meant to do that, Ant!" she admonished me, and I apologized but she said it was OK and not to worry about it. That's as much as I can remember.

'Your book is so true in every way; like you say in your book, ask them to come and make sure the setting is right. I did this and invited Mrs B, even though I couldn't see her I knew she was there, so I told her about Judy and asked if she could give her some signs.

'Just before the end of the holiday, Judy told me that Ruth had lost a small ankle bracelet and hat. Judy was sad about this and she went on to say so. For some reason I opened some magazines in Judy's hotel room and out popped the ankle bracelet, and the next day the hat reappeared there as well. I told Judy I believed it was a message from her mum, and that for some reason she was unable to make dream contact at the moment. Ruth's hat and ankle bracelet were last seen in our room, so how do you think they got to Judy's room (which was at the other side of the hotel)?' – ANTHONY

In my books I suggest asking deceased loved ones to visit in dreams – or at least to try, and if they are unable to reach us, to visit other family members in dream visitations (with permission) instead! I've found that it helps if you speak to a photograph of the deceased (preferably one with a happy memory) or, failing this, hold an item that belonged to them while you think about them. Some people manage perfectly well by conjuring up the face of the deceased and speaking to that vision in their mind. You could also write the deceased loved one a letter of invitation, requesting a visit. Good luck.

A Fond Farewell

'*My story starts in September 1990. It was the evening before I started university and I was working my last shift in a local pub, in a little village about eight miles from Chester. I remember the pub for many reasons, but this night more than any other.*

'*I'd been working in the pub since the age of 13. I started in the kitchen and then later waited on tables. Once I reached 18 I began working behind the bar. It was a great way for me to earn money to keep my pony! Mum and Dad bought him for me on the condition that I'd work to pay for him. He was my birthday present and, although they were prepared to pay for his stabling and grazing, they said I had to pay for his upkeep. It was a great lesson for me, because it taught me the true value of things… and, boy, did I value that pony! Working in the pub was also a fantastic experience. It taught me a lot about life and I met some lovely people.*

'*One of those people was Andy. Andy was a pub regular and we got to know each other quite well. He was a really lovely and genuine bloke… a bit rough round the edges on first meeting, but a great energy and incredibly polite. He walked me home from the pub on a few occasions when we'd had a lock-in, even though I lived five miles from the pub and he lived another three miles from me! He would never accept a lift home from my dad, as he didn't want to inconvenience him! He was always laughing and joking. He loved to enjoy life, going out on his bike, socializing with his friends, clubbing, playing pool, drinking… a little bit too much at times! There was more than one occasion when* it came to locking-up time and Andy seemed to have gone, only to be found asleep under the pool table! He loved the group Queen. If I got any hassle off pub patrons, locals or passers-through, he would come to my defence.

'He was average height... about 5 foot 10, medium build, with short, dark hair and a round (but not chubby) face. Eyes that sparkled with humour and mischief, and a mouth that always seemed to be smiling! He was a very good-looking bloke! He was a person who enjoyed tinkering with his bikes... he was in to mechanics. He had a great sense of humour and a joy for living.

'Andy had just bought a new motorbike and on this particular night he offered to take another friend out for a spin. Andy lent his helmet to his friend and borrowed a helmet from another regular, Michael. Unbeknownst to us at the time, this helmet had a hairline fracture in it.

'The guys went out for the ride and then a couple of hours later Andy's friend staggered back into the bar. He seemed disorientated and when we asked him where Andy was, he looked confused and said, "I don't know."

'Because we were all worried, one of the regulars decided to go out in his car to look for Andy, but a short while later he phoned from the local accident and emergency unit to say there had been an accident... Andy was dead! As you can, imagine we were all in shock! I was in the middle of pulling a pint and I just dropped the whole thing on the floor!

'I found his passing very hard to accept; he was only 20 years old and at this point I didn't really believe in life after death. How could someone so young and full of life suddenly be nothing and cease to exist?

'Well, after that, to say I went off the rails is an understatement! I adopted the attitude, "I could be dead tomorrow," and although I didn't really believe in life after death, I coped by writing Andy letters and then burning them. When I say I went off the rails, I drank far too much. I spent most of my time drunk and I didn't care what people thought about me. I couldn't keep up with my workload at university and, consequently, I failed my first year. I was in a real mess. Andy's death had shaken me up so much I was really struggling to cope.

'Anyway, a few months later I was in bed asleep. I'd gone to bed slightly earlier than usual and it was then that I had a dream about Andy. It was so vivid that when I woke up the next morning I could have sworn it had actually happened! I was in the pub, in the lounge area as a customer, but as I used to work at the pub I thought I'd pop into the kitchen to say "Hi." I dreamed I walked into the kitchen, only it looked slightly different from how it had in real life.

'As I walked into the kitchen I was aware of how quiet and empty it was, and there were lots of shadows. When I looked towards the opposite wall, that whole area brightened and I saw Andy sitting up on the window ledge. He was higher than me so I had to look up to see him, and I can remember feeling confused because he shouldn't have been there! Andy had died, so how could he be in the kitchen? I actually said this to him and he replied that yes, he had passed, but he had also come to chat with me to let me know he was OK, that he didn't suffer as his passing had been pretty much instantaneous. He told me he was happy where he was and had accepted what had happened and he was also at peace. Andy said I had to stop beating myself up about his death and to begin living my life again. This was a real conversation!

'Andy was aware of my sadness, anger and inability to accept what had happened to him. He told me I wasn't to blame for his stupidity! He'd made a bad decision by overshooting the junction and he'd paid for it! He asked me to let him go and to start living my life and enjoying myself. He told me that he would always be around, and suggested I remember the good times.

'We then spent a while talking about other things, which I can't recall now, but when I woke up the next morning I felt happier, lighter and more positive. I knew that what had happened wasn't an ordinary dream. In fact, when I woke up I half-expected to be in the kitchen still talking to him because it was so real! It took me a few moments to remember that he'd died.

'I think Andy came to me that night because although we weren't "best friends", we did have a very close connection. We hit it off right from the first meeting. We had a lot in common and just "clicked". I was very fond of him. I think he knew in some way that his death had affected me badly, and he seemed keen to help me through it.

'I still think of him often, but now it's with happy memories rather than regretful, angry ones, and I don't occupy my thoughts with him every day. I know this was a real visitation experience from his soul rather than a regular dream, and I treasure it even now, many years later.

'Since Andy's passing I believe that life goes on beyond this plane of existence. I believe that we are constantly evolving and learning as a soul. Life is like a play, each decade a scene, and each lifetime an act. The bit in-between is when we return to the consciousness, this is our interval, our time to reflect and allow the other actors their time to shine.

'Andy's visit gave me enormous peace of mind and helped me to move on. It let me realize that there is more than just this plane of existence, and that in some form he lives on. My initial problem had been that it just felt so unfair that he'd died so young when he was so full of life. I found it hard to accept that all of a sudden in the blink of an eye that energy and effervescence could cease to exist. His visit made me realize that it didn't cease; his energy and effervescence still exist, just on another plane. Just because I can't physically see him, it doesn't mean he isn't around. It was definitely a real visit! Even then I knew it wasn't a "normal" dream. It was too vivid and real. Illogical but totally logical all at the same time!

'Strangely enough, a couple of weeks ago I started to think of Andy again, and the alarm on my partner's car started going off at night for no reason! My partner is a psychic and is starting a tour with two other psychic mediums, and one of these mediums picked up a message for me from Andy. He'd come to say hi and let me know how fond of me he still is. My partner asked if Andy was the one setting off the car alarm and, if so, could he please stop! Guess what? Since that day the car alarm hasn't gone off once! Typical Andy, always the joker!

'I honestly don't know why he has come to mind again!
I do periodically think of him, and always with fondness.
Perhaps it's because I am in a new relationship after a long
and bitter divorce four years ago. I'm engaged, expecting
my first baby and incredibly happy! I am doing really well
with my work. I work three days a week for the NHS as
a podiatrist, and three days for myself, doing the podiatry,
reflexology, Indian head and face massage and other therapies.

'I definitely believe in angels! I believe we all have
at least one guardian angel, an angel who is only ever a
thought away. I also believe we are all ONE. We are here to
learn certain lessons that we have chosen before incarnating
into this life. I believe that everyone we meet in life has a
part to play in teaching us those lessons, even the people
who treat us unfairly or aggressively. There are no chance
meetings or events. Of course we have free will, but we all
end up exactly where we are meant to be, when we are
meant to be there.

'I believe that when we pass over it is not the end,
rather an interim before a new beginning. A time for us to
reflect on our journey, the lessons learned, the new questions
posed. A time to heal any hurts suffered and to thank
those who inflicted those hurts upon us for the lessons they
taught and the strength it gave us. I think that rather than
mourning a passing we should celebrate it! Give thanks
for the life that was, the memories that live on and the
knowledge that our loved one has been reconnected to the
biggest source of unconditional love we will ever know!

'And Andy? His death taught me to live each day to
the full because we never know what's round the corner.

To appreciate every experience we have, good or bad. To look at things as if through the eyes of a child and never to take anyone or anything for granted. His visit primarily opened me up to spirit and let me know that life does go on. This in turn gives me hope for the future of the planet. It has given me curiosity to find out more about spirit, angels and to discover a more holistic way of life. It nurtured my inner sense of being a free spirit, and allowed me to follow my heart and be who I am meant to be.

'Along the way I got a bit lost for a while, but even out of that I have learned so much and come back much stronger than before! I think the visitation experience helped me enormously at the time, because it enabled me to move on, free from guilt, regret and anger. It helped get me back on track with my studies so I could complete my course.

'Every event has a domino effect. My work has opened up a lot of doors for me, given me opportunities I may otherwise not have had. It's introduced me to people I would not have met and contributed to making me who I am today. That in turn is shaping who I am yet to become! I think part of this domino effect is that now, looking back on my life thus far, I can honestly say there isn't a single thing I would change. Not even the darkest times! Could I say this if the experience with Andy had never happened? Probably not – he has contributed to everything. Every day I count my blessings and give thanks for everything I have and everything that is yet to come.' – **Helen**

This next story came in an e-mail.

Signs from a Beloved Friend

*'I have been reading your books for almost two years now.
Once I start reading them I just can't seem to put them
down. Your books have given me great inspiration and
helped me with the sudden death of a dear friend. I would
like to share my angel experiences with you.*

*'One of my dearest friends was killed tragically in a
horrific car accident almost three years ago. He was 25 years
of age and was driving along the motorway when the car
lost control and span off the road. The passenger in the car,
who was not wearing a seatbelt, was thrown through the
front windscreen, but my friend, who was driving and had
his seatbelt on, was trapped in the car as it caught fire. This
was a terrible shock and I had to come to terms with losing
one of my closest friends whom I either saw or spoke to
every day.*

*'Just two weeks prior to the accident I had such a vivid
dream that I told my parents about it. I dreamed that
someone had set my car on fire in a petrol station and there
was nothing I could do to stop it. The following week, just
days before my friend's accident, I had another dream where
I was driving my car down a road and the car span out into
mid-air. I managed to jump out unhurt and the car span
through the air, landing in a field opposite. I did not relate
any of this to my friend's accident until my dad reminded
me of the dreams I had shared with them.*

*'For several months following my friend's death I went
to various psychic mediums, searching for confirmation that
he was in heaven and was not suffering or in any pain.
Almost every medium informed me that my friend was*

safe on the other side and was in no pain; they all said he wanted to tell me that he loved me, was with me and that he did not suffer in the accident as he had died on impact. This was very hard, as I missed him so much, but I was so glad that he had reached the other side, was no longer suffering and did not suffer in the accident.

'Since then I came across your angel books and have continued to read them regularly. They have given me great inspiration and have really helped me cope with my friend's death.

'Reading your books and learning of real-life angel experiences has made me recognize signs from the angels and my friend. On the first anniversary of his death I was working the nightshift (in a hospital ward). At midnight my colleague plugged in the computer and on doing this the radio, which was NOT plugged in at the time, came on playing The Beatles' song, "All You Need Is Love." I then read a phrase from this song in one of your books and hoped it was a sign that it was my friend there that night. Several other things happened the same night, like my phone ringing twice then cutting off but there being no missed calls listed on my phone and no name or number coming up while it was ringing, pieces of equipment moving across the room, etc., which as you can imagine terrified my colleagues as they were sceptics.

'On the second anniversary of my beloved friend's death, I was working the dayshift in the hospital. The nurse buzzer system, which is not required for the category of patients in the unit I was working in, started going off. The other staff in the unit could not understand how this was happening, as the buzzers were never used and the buttons were in a place on the wall where no one could have pressed them. The electricians were called out by the ward manager; they checked the system and looked at her strangely, stating that the buzzers had not been touched and the system was working perfectly. This happened intermittently throughout my shift and it made me smile inside, knowing my dear friend was with me.

'There have been various times while I have been on shift in the hospital that patients have asked me who the young man or boy standing behind me is. When I have looked around there has not been one person in sight. Again you could say it was a coincidence, although I hope it has been my friend with me.

'My beloved friend used to call me "angel" all the time. I never thought anything of this at the time, because I just thought it was an affectionate name. The Christmas before his accident I was again working the nightshift in the hospital, when he came in with my Christmas present. This was a wonderful surprise as I did not expect to see him that night. He gave me a few presents, one of which was a book. As I was working over the festive season, I did not have a chance to start reading the book. His accident was in the January and I picked up the book one night to remind me of him. It was then I noticed the title of the book: Remember Me! I felt a cold shiver and my glass beside me began making a sort of tinkling noise. I just thought this was due to his passing being recent, until I became aware of real-life experiences.

'I find white feathers, of all sizes, in all different places. I keep them in a gold cherub box I keep beside my bed, which my mum (who has been my rock throughout this) gave me. I would not have recognized this as a sign until I read your books.

'Many times when I have been feeling down or crying, my pictures of him and me together have moved. One night I was very upset and just wanted to speak to him, one last time. I dried my eyes and walked into my room, and there on the bed was the last picture ever taken of the both of us, which had been pinned up on my wall. This made me feel his presence and warmth again.

'One night I had the most vivid dream where my friend was walking me home from work (I normally drive as it's too far too walk). We were walking for a long time, chatting. When we reached the gates of my house he cuddled me tight, kissed me and said, "I have to go now, angel." I begged him to stay and kept saying, "I have so much to tell you," but he slowly faded away.

'In the dream I was crying so hard and felt so much hurt. When I woke up I was still crying, though throughout the day I began to feel some peace and felt so lucky to have had another chance to be with my dear friend. He also had the same outfit on that he had on in the last photo taken of us both. I have since had dreams where he is with me, talking to me, but none as vivid and real as that first one. In every other dream he has been wearing the exact same clothes he had on the last time I saw him before he died. I would like to believe this is not coincidence.

'My gran, who has been very unwell for the past few years and is very confused, speaks of my grandfather regularly, telling my mum, "Your dad's here" or "Your dad's just left." She speaks to him regularly and is always telling me about the boy who stands next to me all the time. When I ask her what he looks like, she tells me "He is dark with beautiful eyes." My friend was Sikh and everyone always commented on his smiling eyes. I believe he is watching over my gran when I'm not there. Several times after she says it and I drive away from her house, my CD player in the car will jump to one of his favourite songs and the volume will go up and down. This gives me a shiver all over and makes me smile, knowing he is there.

'One medium I went to see said to me as soon as I walked in the door, "There are two men who've just walked in with you, your grandfather from your mother's side and a young man, tall, dark and with big smiling eyes, wearing something on his head. They both watch over you." I was so shocked at how accurate this description was. As I stated above, my friend was of the Sikh religion and always wore a bandana to cover his head. I knew he would always be with me, as would my grandfather (even though I never met him).

'I had a terrible time at work with my boss. My friend used to come up to see me on my breaks to cheer me up; he would always say "You're good at your job, and if I'm ever in hospital I would want you to look after me," then cuddle me. This situation at work got worse after he died, and there were many times I just wanted to run away from work. I love my job but couldn't take any more bullying. Every time I felt like running away, I would almost see an image of my dearest friend in front of me, smiling and saying the exact same words he always said. This somehow gave me the strength to smile and carry on with my work; my day always seemed to brighten up when this happened.

'Recently I have been unwell, with breathing problems. One night I nearly had to attend hospital, though prayed to my dear friend and angels to watch over me. Throughout the night it became easier to breathe and I thanked my friend and angels. While in bed that night, I heard three knocks on my bedroom door. I got up out of bed and went into the hall, where my brother was just coming up the stairs. When I asked him if he had chapped my door, he looked at me strangely and told me I was imagining things. Once again I smiled and felt great warmth that this may have been a sign.

'I would like to thank you for all your inspiration. I would like to believe these experiences were not coincidences, and hope these were visitations and signs from my beloved friend.' – CLAIRE

Stories of Psychic Children

'…a dream that became a reality
and spread throughout the stars.'
WILLIAM SHATNER AS CAPTAIN JAMES T. KIRK IN THE
1969 *STAR TREK* EPISODE 'WHOM GODS DESTROY'

We've mentioned psychic children in the Introduction, but I wanted to share a couple of stories with you here in depth. Remember, there are thousands of children being born with these types of skills all around the world at the moment!

Little Psychic Girl

'My young daughter Emilia was in our local evening paper around three years ago because of her psychic abilities. She is now six and still talks to her "sky friends" as she calls them. A while ago a friend brought a psychic round to the house with her and the psychic told me my daughter was extremely gifted, too, but we were already aware of her

talents. The expert told me it was likely that Emilia would stop seeing spirit around the age of five, but that time has been and gone and she still sees them everywhere we go.

'She used to chat to an old man and two little boys in our house, but usually she keeps quiet about what she is doing. She sees someone called Michael a lot. If she wants to talk to me about any of her friends I just listen or say, "Mmm, that's nice, love," because I've found that if family and friends are around and I ask Emilia to tell them what Michael has said she would get very defensive and say I was telling fibs. It was as if nobody else was allowed to know about the spirits she sees. Michael, she tells me, is her "boyfriend from the sky". She talks to Michael constantly, and has done so for as long as I can remember.

'When she was very little she would point very excitedly and say, "old man!" and wave frantically to thin air. Everywhere we went she would see this old man, so I decided because of this it must be her guardian angel. I asked the psychic if this could this be true, but she told me it wasn't an angel but simply spirits my daughter was seeing. Emilia was too young to understand who he was and just continued to call him "old man". Because the old man was always in the house I asked the psychic to bless the house so he would leave. The very next day my daughter knew he was gone; she just picked up on it and told me, "The old man lives in the sky now." After the old man left, Michael appeared. At first she always said he was naughty and swore, but he seems to have calmed down a lot now, and is helpful rather than annoying. Sometimes we don't hear from him in ages and Emilia says that Michael has been with his dad.

'Emilia is starting to understand more about the phenomenon now, and realizes that only she can see Michael. Recently we were watching a film called Drop Dead Fred *about a girl who has an "imaginary" friend nobody else can see. Emilia commented, "Aw, Mam, she's the same as me."*

'None of her school friends knows about her abilities, but the teachers have known about her from the start. The doctors used to say she has "absence seizures" (where she goes into a daydream-like trance state and no matter what you do she doesn't come out it. Her eyes just glaze over). She's had lots of tests/scans for this and they all come back fine. The psychic told me she thinks there is nothing medically wrong with Emilia and explained that this is when she communicates with the other side. It seems she's probably right.

'Emilia is a lovely little girl and her abilities don't seem to bother her in any way. She makes friends with anyone and is a very bubbly character; she always seems to be happy when she's talking to her "sky friends". Emilia knew when I was pregnant even before I did. She was very persistent about it and in the end I did a pregnancy test and discovered that, much to my surprise, she was right.

'She sometimes stops random strangers to give them messages. Once my neighbours took her to the supermarket with them (Emilia plays with their granddaughter). When they brought her back they said to me, "My, what a queer kid you've got!" and laughed. Apparently there was an old gentleman in the café and Emilia approached him and said, "You've got lots of medals because you used to fly a plane with a man called...", and then she gave his name, and the old man replied, "Eee, how do you know that?" and he confirmed that what she'd said was true.

'Although my daughter was in the local paper, not a lot of people know she's special (they've either forgotten or didn't read the feature). We don't usually talk about it because I don't want her to be judged or made to feel different in any way, especially around other children.

'A few months ago she said to me, "Aw, Nana Joan passed away on Thursday at home." Later that evening we got an e-mail from Joan's daughter saying exactly those words. It was strange but wonderful. As Emilia grows up, I wonder if she'll continue to bring people messages from the other side. Whatever happens, I'm very proud of my daughter.' – CHARLENE

This next story came as a letter from a friend. I have her permission to use the story here, although for the sake of her privacy I have changed the names of the people involved.

Blessed Twice by Angel Michael

'I've a lovely true story you might be interested in. I met a girl called Mary, who I knew from years ago, in the shop last week, pushing a pram and holding a wee boy's hand. She and her husband had been trying for a baby for 12 years but it wasn't to be. They decided to adopt in Northern Ireland, but because of the length of time it was taking decided to go to London.

'They found a beautiful little boy aged two, named Adam, and set the wheels in motion. At their first meeting with the little boy he ran over to Mary, hugged her and told her she was going to be his mum. Months went by and Social Services back here in Northern Ireland were dragging their heels, so Mary went to Social Services, lifted her files and forwarded them to London by registered post. They were approved in a few months and arrangements were made for the little boy to come over with his care parents for the hand-over.

'When a hand-over happens the carers and child usually go to a hotel for a few days so that they can take it slowly to make sure both are happy, but not in this case. When the little boy came out of Arrivals he ran and jumped into Mary's arms, saying "Mummy, I am coming home with you now" – and that's exactly what he did. The family were delighted, so happy, their dreams had come true.

'One night the little boy said to Mary that he would like a baby sister, and told Mary that they would be getting a little girl. Mary, knowing that she couldn't have children, dismissed his comment. After a few months he said it again, and told her that "Michael said" she would be getting a baby girl. A month later Mary found out she was pregnant. The little boy told everyone that his mummy was having a little girl; as a result his teacher congratulated Mary, saying how lovely it was that she was having a little girl. (At that point, Mary didn't know the sex of the baby.)

'One day while Mary and Adam were playing, he looked up into the air and said, "Look, Mummy, there's Michael!" Mary asked Adam what Michael looked like, and Adam described him as being very big with a sword.

Jacky, as I was listening I got goosebumps. I asked Adam about Michael and if he looks after him, and he said yes, he plays with him. It was so normal for him!! So Mary has a healthy beautiful little girl who was born safe and sound, and Mary went from having had no family for so long to having two beautiful children. What do you think of that?!' – **K**

Stories of Protection

'There shall no evil befall thee, neither shall any plague come nigh thy dwelling. For he shall give his angels charge over thee, to keep thee in all thy ways. They shall bear thee up in their hands, lest thou dash thy foot against a stone.'

PSALMS 91:10–12

So many of the stories readers send me are about angels protecting them. These stories are amazing and wonderful, and I knew they would be perfect here.

The Car Angels

'I have always believed in angels, and my first angel experience happened when I was about 13 years old. My grandmother, who has since passed away, must have tried every religion possible and, being like a second mother to me, she taught me about religion and angels from a very young age.

'I moved to America when I was just 11 years old so that the family could live with my American stepfather. On a hot summer's day in 1983, my mother Kathryn, stepfather Marc, my younger brother Chris and I all went on a family day out. We were travelling from home, which was in Cheney, Kansas. The journey was about half an hour to our destination, Cheney Reservoir: a beautiful beach with a sandy area and a nice lake for fishing and swimming. We had a wonderful day sunbathing, and even took a picnic. It was a normal family event but what happened next was to change my life forever.

'After our lovely day out, we jumped back into the car to drive the short distance home. We were excitedly talking about our day and what fun we'd had, when we accidently ran a red light at an intersection. It was a busy crossroads with two lanes in every direction, a little like a dual carriageway. It was terrifying: to the left and to the right of us we had trucks as well as cars turning from the road ahead. We didn't stand a chance; it was too late to brake or stop. As I looked ahead I could see a lorry coming straight for us. There was no way out. Stopping, reversing, speeding up… it wouldn't have made a difference.

'All four of us in the car closed our eyes and prepared for impact. The last thing I recall at this stage was asking for God to help us. Then, all of a sudden time seemed to stop and we were aware that our car was being lifted into the air; it was like a slow-motion floating sensation, as if a giant pair of hands had lifted the car up into the air. The next thing we knew we were safe and unharmed on the other side of the intersection, just driving along normally!

'As soon as he could do so my step-dad pulled the car over to a safe spot a little further up the road. We were all dumbstruck! It all happened so fast that we couldn't work out what had happened! My brother and I had been screaming from the backseat, and I was still silently begging for God to not kill us. My step-dad was cursing out of fright and my mum was praying loudly.

'One second we were screaming and praying, and the next we were safely through the traffic. I'd already figured that if I was going to die I might as well close my eyes, because I knew it would be quick. But something had carried us away from harm. The landing was soft. There is no way another car pushed us; I know this because I have been in a serious car accident since this one. There was no damage to our vehicle, no loud metal-on-metal sound, and no other possible answer. We just knew we'd been protected by angels, even though it's hard to explain. You don't have to see, but we know what we felt, and we felt and experienced a "time-freeze", like in a film. We were now breathing with relief and we all looked at each other with a knowledge of what we'd all been though together. If other drivers noticed, no one stopped to say, and after calming down we just carried on home.

'Mum and I still mention that day from time to time. I think my brother and step-dad aren't so vocal about it but I've also shared it with my boyfriend and friends. I'm pleased to talk about it because it proves there is something else out there. Things like that don't happen every day, so how can you not believe?

'Years later I was in another car accident; I was alone in the backseat of the car and my mother was in the driver's seat. A car hit us with such force that it moved our car into some trees. Strangely, I was unhurt again. I had just bought a television set, which I'd put on the right-hand side in the backseat with me. Normally I sit on the right. Anyway, the whole of the right-hand side of the boot was pushed into the back seat on impact, and I realized right away that if I had been sitting there I would have been killed.

'At the time I'd been suffering from depression and spent many weeks in bed. One night an amazingly bright light appeared at my bedroom window. It was so bright that I was squinting. At the window stood an angel about seven or eight feet tall at least; he had long hair and huge wings and he smiled at me before walking away. I got up and could see "wing" prints in the snow. I told my nan about it the next morning and she said she had seen the same angel a few times, and in the same way, at her window. Needless to say, my depression passed after that!' – HELEN

Snow Patrol

'Did I believe in angels? Well, in all honesty probably not; I thought they were no more than fantasy or wishful thinking. Did I believe in spirits? Yes, as dead relatives helping out from beyond… maybe.

'My mother and I have always shared a strong spiritual bond; we are very close and often think alike. As I grew into my teenage years we would go and visit Spiritualist mediums together; we shared a common interest in "this sort of thing". We both became more aware of spirit energy 20 *years ago, around the time of her mother's death (my beloved Granny Cashon).*

'*Before my granny's passing we would see shadows move around in the house. Three days after her passing Granny Cashon visited me in the middle of the night; she touched my arm to wake me, then spoke to me in her normal voice. This was the spark that lit the flame, and I have been interested in this sort of phenomenon ever since. I have sat in Spiritualist church psychic development circles in the past, but to be honest hadn't done much with angels until having the urge to purchase dozens of books with some redundancy money two years ago (2009). This was when I discovered angels were actually real, after reading books by several well-known authors... including yours. Reading the books changed my life somewhat, and I even ask for angels to help me every day now... but one day they proved to me they were real. I believe an angel saved my life.*

'*My partner John and I have a daughter, Erin, who was two years old at the time. We did everything back-to-front, really, because we had our house and children before getting married (we finally married in 2008 after 13 years together!). John was a sales rep and covered all of Northern Ireland and Scotland, including the Shetlands, so he was often away from Monday until Friday!*

'*Snow fell in the area around our house one winter. It was beautiful and I was very much aware that this was little Erin's first experience of snow and I was keen to take her out to explore. John was away, so as it was my day off I decided that I could show Erin lots and lots of snow if we took a 40-minute drive north to the Trossachs, a very rural* forest area near Callander. Without thinking too much about it I strapped Erin into the car, picked up a take-away from the drive-thru for lunch, and set off... totally unprepared. I had high-heeled fashion boots on and in the rush had left my mobile phone in the house. Nobody knew what our plans were, and as I write this I can see what a big mistake I'd made.

'As we drove along the snow got thicker and it became more and more tricky to drive the closer we got to Callander, but still I continued. Erin was so excited with all the white stuff and I didn't want to disappoint her. Eventually we turned off the main road, taking the route uphill towards the lochs and forested areas (needless to say, nobody else was doing the same thing because the weather was now so bad). I drove a fair distance, but as we continued I started to panic a little. I truly was on the road of no return. The ground was completely white with thick snow... exciting, but I was on a narrow track and the wheels of the car had begun to spin. The only way was up.

'I remember being in such a panic and feeling such a fool for compromising the safety of myself and Erin. I often talk to myself or sing along to the radio in the car; I began asking for help in my mind as the car slithered about the track in the snow. It was so scary, but I have no idea who I thought would come to help me; I just wanted to get out of the situation.

'Time went on and I was in quite a panic now. I had no phone, no jacket, I hadn't told anyone where we were going, I had silly inappropriate footwear on and now it was starting to get dark. I wondered about abandoning the car

in the middle of nowhere and walking into the town with
Erin, but I couldn't abandon the car in the middle of the
road! I was way too scared to leave the car in case it blocked
the way for someone else, so the only thing I could do was to
keep persevering with the car up the hill in the hope that I
might be able to turn the car around somehow. Our passage
was slow, the wheels were spinning with the icy, slippery
snow underneath and, worse, I had no idea what was up the
hill and no idea where I was going. I just continued to pray
as hard as I could while driving very, very slowly.

'Suddenly right in front of us a huge jeep appeared,
creeping towards us from the road ahead. It was travelling
down the hill as we were travelling up. By the time I saw
it I was already stuck in the snow… I was going nowhere
and had now blocked the path, and the jeep had no way of
getting past us.

'The occupants of the jeep, a man and a woman, got
out so I got out, too, and made my way over to them to tell
them how silly I'd been. I recall the woman saying to me,
"Of course you have your mobile phone with you…?"
And I said yes, even though it was a lie, because I felt too
humiliated to tell her I hadn't!

'Strangely they didn't judge me; instead they offered
help. The man got into my car to move it for me. Erin was
still strapped to her car seat, but I wasn't concerned. I stood
with the woman and it was only at this time I noticed the
sheer drop next to the track. It looked very scary to me, but
the man didn't seem troubled. He turned my car around
very efficiently, pointing it downhill; to me he did it with
such ease, but it must have been a 20-point turn! At no

point was I afraid; if anything I felt strangely calm, as actually there was something very serene about the whole situation. Erin was happy to be in the car with him, too.

'After thanking them most sincerely I returned to the car with my contented daughter. I gathered my thoughts for a second before starting the engine. Then I pulled away and, as I looked up to wave in the mirror, the couple were nowhere to be seen! I was completely confused because they had been on their way down the hill at the time they found me. I hadn't heard them pull away from me, and to have disappeared they had either reversed back up the hill, which seemed a dangerous thing to do, or done a 20-point turn in their jeep as the man had just done for me! I was completely bemused! I can't see why they would have turned around and gone back the way they came; they must have been coming downhill for a reason, surely? I've got goosebumps even now thinking back, but I also felt excited and couldn't wait to get back to my mum's to tell her all about it. Who had helped me?

'I drove slowly and carefully on the drive to Mum's, and luckily the rest of the journey was uneventful. When I arrived, the first thing I did was tell her how incredibly stupid I'd been going out with Erin, especially as I was so unprepared. I wanted to cry actually because I felt so mad with myself and embarrassed that I could have been reading about myself in the newspapers having been rescued by the police or a mountain rescue team… at the cost of thousands of pounds. I was just so humbled by what could have happened had we not been "rescued". After feeling so calm, the reality of the situation suddenly hit me.

'Mum, on the other hand, was delighted because we'd made it back home safely and also that someone or something had intervened. I remember us standing looking at one another with big eyes in that sort of "knowing" way. I still don't know to this day whether I think the couple were angels or whether they were sent by the angels. I suppose if they were angels then they had every right to just disappear into the air; if they were an ordinary couple out for a drive in the snow, then they would definitely have been driving behind us as we drove off... so I guess they were angels!

'I was so mad at myself, I have often read in newspapers and heard on the news about people (like me) who had gone out totally unprepared for bad weather, and yet this very day I had been that person about whom you always say, "Why would someone do such a thing?" I had wanted to show Erin her first snow, but I could have cost us our lives. I definitely won't be so foolish ever again. I believe everything happens for a reason and this life is a learning process. I guess the experience didn't quite change my life at the time... however, since reading about angels over the past couple of years I now wish I could go back in time and absorb every piece of information the couple were willing to give. How awesome. I feel so loved.

'It was another five years or more before I immersed myself in angels with books and figurines, etc. It may sound daft, but I've always felt protected throughout my life, and even more so now that I have a strong connection with angels in my daily life.

'Erin is now ten and has been joined by Teagan, who is five. Both girls are spiritual and I think it's just magical to be able to talk to them about spirits and angels without any fear. John is now disabled but he too regularly asks the angels for assistance and they never let him down… he's always sure to thank them. We have all been given a white feather at one time or another, and as well as knowing the angels are around us all I know Erin and I were saved by angels on a day I shall never forget.' – **ANGELINA**

My Angel Michael Saved My Life

'I had a car accident on 17 May 1982. I was at a friend's house when one of their children kicked a cup of hot chocolate all over my white jeans. At the time we were on our way out to the cinema, so I jumped into my little green car and raced home to change my clothes.

'I had only a short journey but on the way back to the house I had an accident. It was a beautiful sunny evening but the road was wet. The drive from the local fruit farm had been washed down, and as my tyre hit a patch of water it immediately went into a skid. My car wheel dropped into a hole in the road and it was then that I lost control of the car. The car flipped right through a fence.

'I was conscious throughout the experience, but when the car came to a stop I realized a post had gone through my body and pinned me to the seat. A 4 x 4 wooden post came right through the door of the car; it had ripped through my jeans and gone right through my stomach, stopping at my hip.

'Strangely, I didn't immediately feel panic… I guess I must have been in shock at the time but I did feel as if someone was with me by this time. Someone or something was helping me. I felt a sort of warmth, like a hug, and it comforted me.

'I think I must have damaged the fuel tank, too, because the smell of petrol was overwhelming. There was a type of "urgency" feeling for me to get out of the car, so I felt for the stake and pushed it out. I really don't think I did this on my own. I knew I was being assisted somehow. Then I moved about ten feet away from the danger of the car.

'I now found myself lying in a field. I had severed the main artery in my legs and had a broken pelvis, so there was no way I could have walked from the car. It was, and still is, a mystery to me.

'The next thing I remember was a man running across the field to help me; he had already called for an ambulance when he heard the crash from the other side of the field. Luckily for me he was an ambulance driver himself, so had some experience in dealing with emergency situations.

'Everyone at the scene commented on how bad my injuries were; I had two police cars and four police motorcycles to get me the 16 miles to the hospital. I really think I could have died in the accident.

'I was taken to hospital, where they also discovered I had ripped my bowel and intestines as well as having many more horrific injuries. I was in the operating theatre for seven hours following the accident. Apparently I died twice, and at one point I can remember seeing myself in theatre and all the doctors around me.

'The first time I died was when I first arrived at the hospital; I felt a pull and I was looking down from the

ceiling at the nurses and doctors running round. One nurse
was cutting off my trousers and T-shirt, which were bright
red. I knew I didn't want to die, but I also had the feeling of
fascination, watching exactly what they were doing. The next
thing I remember was when I was on the operating table; I
was examining my own body as they removed part of my
bowel and intestine, and stitching my face. Then I could
hear the doctors saying they were losing me and I remember
thinking that I wasn't going to let that happen, and that
feeling of warmth as someone or something was helping me
back. I can also remember talking to someone called Michael
during the procedure when I was unconscious.

'I believed then and now that Michael was an angel
taking care of me. He stayed with me all the time, holding
me; I felt as if he was holding on to my life-force and not
going to let me go. I could hear all the sirens and felt the
speed at which I was being driven to hospital, but all the
time he kept me calm and he told me to stay awake.

'It was a horrific experience and I was told at the time
that I would probably never walk again and never have
children. But I knew I was being helped by my angel that
day. Clearly I still had important work to do on Earth. I
certainly believe in angels and I think I am living proof that
Archangel Michael saved my life that day. I still believe he
is with me. The best thing that came out of that day was
my daughter. I was told I would never carry a child after my
injuries, and most of all I would probably would never walk
again. It was 29 years ago today, and my daughter is now
13. I have my own horse; I taught myself to ride again after
the accident, and I have four lovely basset hounds and a little

mongrel. They are all rescue dogs. My life changed completely that day and I am sure it made me a better person.

'...*Oh, and I've never been in a green car since!*' – **HAYLEY**

Archangel Michael is a very busy guy indeed. He appears in story after story. It's clear how he is one of the most important angels to work with human beings. He talks to children, aids in rescues and offers comfort. Never believe that angels aren't real... of course they are real!

Pet Stories

'Lots of people talk to animals...
Not very many listen, though... That's the problem.'
BENJAMIN HOFF, *THE TAO OF POOH*

Many of my books contain paranormal stories relating to pets. Our animals are boundless energies of unconditional love; their love never ends when the body passes to the other side. I know that these pet stories are very special to my readers, so I wanted to include one or two here for you.

My Precious Dog Came Back to Me

'We never knew Belle's age exactly, but we believed she was around 14 when she passed away. Belle was such a special dog, a Nova Scotia Duck-Tolling Retriever mix. My husband-to-be and I had just got together when she came into our lives, a new, fresh relationship... it was 1998.

'One day we were driving around with no specific place to go. We drove by a small town where a little private festival was taking place. Bands were playing and it looked such fun that we decided to stop. In the crowd I spotted this little cute dog, but it was dirty, thin, shy and begging for hot dog leftovers. My heart melted immediately. I started to ask questions about her, and discovered she was a stray. Belle used to hang around the bar where the festival was taking place. The bar owner was fed up with her begging and had already decided to have her put down. I talked to my partner and we decided to give her a chance at life. We packed her up in the car with us and took her home that very day.

'Animals always have been a big part of my life. At that time, I just wanted to give her a second chance and save her life. When we brought her home I knew right away that she had been mistreated. She was afraid of everything and she didn't have faith in herself or anybody. She trusted nobody. I'd had a rough life myself… so I looked into her eyes and I told her, "I know what you went through. I'm going to help you find your strength again and your trust in people. I'm going to love you with all that I have, and give you the life you deserve."

'And so the journey with Belle began. In no time she gained her trust in the people who surrounded her and was just the perfect girl. Belle was always making us laugh and giving us love in the way only she knew how to give. She was amazing in every way. She was always there for me when I needed her the most. She was my confidante, my best friend and always by my side.

'Belle looked like an angel. She was cream in colour, with white markings on the tip of her four paws and a white spot on her chest. She used to make us laugh when she played with her plush squeaky duck. She just loved that little duck, though I never really understood why.

'Belle had grown in confidence but she was still a shy little girl. She really loved to play, and turned every moment of the day into a game. Even with her food, I had to throw her kibbles so that she would run and catch them. Loving us was her goal in life. She loved giving us kisses and she knew how to make us laugh. She used to do a strange thing with her ears that I used to call her "mouse ears". When I asked her to make the "mouse ears", she would and it made us laugh and laugh. Like many dogs, she loved a belly massage. It didn't matter how many times you did it for her, it was never enough and she always asked for more.

'Every moment with Belle was a blessing in every way. I told her several times that she was an angel sent from above. We went through everything together. We have so many memories with her: the walks, the games, the vacations, the rides, the talks… at Christmas she would let us make a fool of her – we used to dress her up in Christmas hats and reindeer ears. She'd give us that look that said, "OK… I'm not enjoying this but I will play along because I know you like it!"

'The best thing of all was to see her overcome her fears. It taught me a lesson that with love, we can overcome anything. Belle taught me to love unconditionally. And because of her, I decided to devote myself to animals. In 2005 my husband and I began a non-profit shelter for cats.

We saved the lives of over 400 cats and some dogs during the time we ran the shelter. Unfortunately, we had to close it in 2008. Lack of help and financial support made it so hard. But we still care for 27 cats we were left with, the older ones who couldn't find a home. Some of them have medical problems like diabetes, but we will never let them down. I now own five dogs, 27 cats and a horse. We're a family.

'Belle was special and she slept in our bed with us. She loved walks and she especially loved to ride with me in my convertible jeep. If I close my eyes I still see her fur and her ears flowing in the air. Later on we found another stray dog, a German Shepherd/Rottweiler mix. We found him in the middle of the highway when he was about four months old. We brought him home and he and Belle became inseparable. Later on we adopted a Basset Hound. And then of course the shelter came. When Belle passed away, my German Shepherd kept searching for her and wasn't himself anymore. Belle had such a kindness about her; there was a special look in her eyes. She had such special love to give and she meant everything to me. A lot of people always told me that animals have no souls. I never believed that.

'It was Christmas of 2007. Belle started to feel weak and not long after that she stopped eating. We rushed her to the vet's and they ran every test they could think of. X-rays revealed that she had a tumour the size of an orange. And that it had spread all over her body. It was too late; there was nothing more they could do. My world fell apart in seconds. I knew someday we'd lose her, but I also knew I would never be ready to let my little girl go. I asked the vet how much time she had left, but because she had already stopped eating we knew it wouldn't be long.

'I asked the vet to give me something for her appetite and brought Belle home. Over the next few days I cooked her special meals, and she did eat small amounts. We both knew she was dying and that we didn't have much time left together. I spoiled her right to the end. The morning of 5 January 2008, I looked into her beautiful eyes and knew right away that it was time to put her suffering to an end. I stayed with her all the way to the vet's, telling her that everything would be all right and that we would be reunited somehow, someday.

'She fell into her eternal sleep right before my eyes; I have never felt pain like it in my whole entire life. I spent the week after that crying like I've never cried before. I would talk to her and look at pictures and remember all the special times we'd had together. I used to sleep with her little duck because it brought me comfort. And that's when I started praying to my angels. The pain was unbearable.

'One night in my prayers I asked the angels to take care of Belle. In my own sadness and in my own selfish needs I asked them if there was a way that they could bring her back to me; I was begging for her to come back. My grieving process was not going well at all. But one night I managed to fall into a deep sleep, and that night I had the first dream. I saw Belle in a glowing light; she was so beautiful. Next to her there was a grey shadow, a male in form with a bright light around him. He spoke to me. He told me, "She's in good hands. I'm going to take care of her and in time I'll bring her back to you…"

'I woke up and was stunned by what happened. I felt such strong feelings of love and peace in my heart and my soul. Right after that I knew I was going to have Belle with me again, and the only way I thought that would be possible would be to have her returned to me in another body with the help of my angels.

'That night, that angel gave me the hope that, yes, this was possible, so the next morning I jumped on my computer and began to search for all the Nova Scotia Duck-Tolling Retriever breeders I could find. I searched and searched, and eventually found a breeder in Ontario (16 hours' drive from where I live). They were expecting two litters in the January, so I contacted them and told them about my loss. One of the litters was already spoken for, but the other litter was still available. And best of all, I would have first pick of the litter. I was thrilled!

'I kept in touch with the breeder every day, a lovely woman originally from England. She sent me pictures of the mother and father of the new puppies to come, and when I saw the mother I was very surprised to see that she looked just like Belle, but in another colour. Time went by and I still missed my little girl, but I was determined to bring her back home. It's the only way I could deal with the grief. But bad days would come often … when the memories surfaced. I would cry and cry.

'One night I had another dream. I saw Belle in the same glowing light with the angel by her side. And she's the one who "spoke" to me that night. She told me, "Mom, stop hurting… I'm coming home…" The next morning I rushed to my computer to check my e-mails, and saw an e-mail from the breeder. She told me that the puppies had been born during the night and that all had gone well. The mom and the babies were all doing great. She sent me a picture of the mom and puppies together. Tears ran down my cheeks. I realized that Belle had come to me during the night before entering her new body. It was now 17 January.

'I had to choose between three little girls. Since I was 16 hours away from the puppies, it was hard for me to go and see them, so the breeder was sending me all the pictures that she could. One night I asked my angels again for help. "How will I know which one to choose?" A few days later I had my third dream. It was the same angel, and he said to me that I would see a sign. As the puppies grew older, the breeder sent me a ton of pictures of the three little girls. One of them was lighter in colour. Belle was a shade of cream, rare for her breed, but I knew Belle was cross-mixed. And when I saw that little girl, light in colour, I knew that was my sign.

'I know I picked the right one. I saw her growing up in the pictures. I recognized the same look in her eyes. The same white markings on the paws and chest... even my mom told me one day, "Look at her eyes, they're the same as Belle's." I told my mom my story a long time after this.

'My little girl came home at eight weeks of age in the March. She flew to Quebec City, which was three hours from where I live. It was the most exciting day ever! When I saw her in her little cage, looking scared, I took her in my arms and I said, "Welcome back, my sweet angel." She was this little fur ball, cute as ever, the most precious, beautiful little girl I've ever seen. We drove her home, stopping often to give her little walks. She was shy but by the third stop, she'd begun to play a little. She was too cute! Back home we introduced her to her brothers and all went well.

'Our new little girl is called Fancy-Divine. Fancy is a little angel, too; she's the sweetest dog. Her face and her personality just melt everyone's heart. She gives a lot of kisses and loves to play… but in her case it's really an obsession. She's a real clown. When we ask her to laugh, she does this thing with her teeth; it's the funniest thing ever. She's the most lovable little girl on Earth. Our lifestyle didn't change when Fancy arrived. We still go for walks, rides, games, vacations – she's in every moment of our lives… and she's my best friend.

'I firmly believe that she is the reincarnation of Belle. There have been so many signs. The first time I gave her food (she was only two months old at the time) was the same day I brought her home. She was looking at her bowl, and looking at me afterwards, the same way Belle did. Belle invited me to play with her and the food that way. It was the same look, the same body position, so I grabbed a kibble and threw it across the floor like I used to do with Belle, and I got exactly the same reaction: she ran to catch it. We did this a little more and she reached her bowl to eat the rest, just like Belle used to do.

'Fancy just turned three years old and still plays with her food. The look in her eyes is the same… I really believe it's the same soul. The same "mouse ears" thing. Same personality except that she's more playful and less shy. I guess that's because she didn't have to put up with any abuse. But she still has her same kindness, her same approach. Belle was not an aggressive dog, but when she was in the car or jeep and we would stop for gasoline, she was scared of whoever was fuelling up and would bark at them. Fancy developed the same reaction with no reason. Me, my husband, my mom and dad, we're convinced that we have Belle back in our lives.

'I believe in angels. I truly believe that they're there to help us in every way they can, and that they can reach out to us if we let them and welcome them into our lives. This experience changed my life. I know I'm not alone. I know my angels surround me in every moment. I feel their love. The universe or other dimensions are full of mysteries. I don't look for answers. I'm just aware that we're not alone, and even though we can't see them, it doesn't mean that angels and paranormal forces don't surround us. What I experienced is real and I thank the angels from the bottom of my heart. They really came to me. And they still do. They're a part of my everyday life.

'My little girl was really back… oh, and I still have that little duck. He has a special place in my house!'

– CHANTALE

Lovely Lucy

'Many years ago when my husband and I first married, we lived in an isolated area and decided it would be to our benefit to own a dog. As I was working a night shift my husband went to the RSPCA to look at the homeless dogs for re-housing. He chose a Boxer-cross Labrador female, and even picked out the name Lucy after Lucille Ball. The next day I was to view this dog to see if she was the right one for us. Thankfully he had done all the spadework, so to speak, because when I went to see her there were that many dogs I would not have had a clue which one to have. I'm sure in my mind I would have come away with more than one dog.

'Lucy proved to be a very special dog, and made friends with the local farmer's dog and all the local animals around. She used to chase the rabbits away so that they couldn't be shot, and would walk down the road with our pig Arnold to meet my husband Hugh from work.

'When I was working late Hugh would often have a few pints in the local pub, which was about a kilometre from our house. Lucy seemed to sense where he was and would wait outside the pub door waiting for someone to come out so she could make a dash inside and sit down beside him, as much as to say "It's time you came home."

'During the shooting season, duck hunters would cross the property next to ours to gain access to the creek that ran through quite a number of properties. On this one day in particular a hunter made the remark that he thought Lucy would probably be a good hunting dog. Little did he know she would more than likely chase the ducks away rather than let them be shot. The next morning Lucy was nowhere to be seen. At first I thought she was with Oliver, the farm dog, as he used to visit her once he had brought the cows in. For three weeks she was missing, and I actually gave up the idea of ever seeing her again. It was a Friday evening when I was searching the local papers for Labrador puppies but nothing was advertised.

'I made myself ready to do the weekly shopping and, just as we went outside to get the car, who should be sitting at the bottom of the steps outside? Lucy! What wonderful thoughts went through my head. "Wow, you are back," I called to her, and encouraged her to climb up the three steps to our door. But it was too much to ask, she just couldn't do it. Her pads were bleeding and the inner part of her legs was all chafed. Hugh carried her inside and we made her as comfortable as possible, but it took her a week to get back on her feet. We couldn't think where or who she'd been with all that time, only that all she wanted was to come home.

'Lucy continued to bring all the stray dogs home, and even found a kitten that she looked after as if it were her own; they used to go everywhere together. Children added to the mix, as by this time we had two of our own. Of course they too were loved by Lucy, and she enjoyed playing with them and watching over them as they did her.

'Sadly the time came when we sold our country property to live in the town to be nearer the schools. Lucy didn't take too kindly to the restrictions and seemed quite sad at times. My sister, who had been suffering with rheumatoid arthritis, had been having gold injections over the past many months. Unbeknownst to the family she was having adverse reactions to the treatment, which even the doctor didn't realize. After the last injection she became really ill and was confined to bed. The doctor would visit daily and was really concerned for her. The next day our beloved Lucy passed away with a heart complaint; we were all devastated because it was so sudden.

'That night Lucy came to visit my sister in a dream. She told her that she had died so that she, my sister, could *live. Lucy indicated to my sister in the dream visit that she didn't mind if I got another dog. Nevertheless it took me 20 years before I could bring myself to own another dog. He also came from the pound, and just like Lucy he is much loved by people and animals alike.'* – VIOLET

Healing and
Heavenly Experiences

*'Healing, Papa would tell me, is not a science,
but the intuitive art of wooing nature.'*
W. H. AUDEN

I've mixed two subjects together here: visits to heaven
and healing encounters. I believe they are equally
magical experiences. See what you think.

During a near-death experience many people visit a
heavenly realm for the briefest of time before they are
turned back by an angel or deceased relative, who tells
them, 'It's not your time.'

In this next story the reader didn't die... at least as
far as we are aware, although she was very ill. These
heavenly encounters are very rare and, therefore, all
the more worth recording. It's not every day you get a
glimpse of a little piece of heaven.

Flying with My Angel

'My name is Tammie and when I was 33 I suddenly
became very ill. After going to my doctor nearly every day for
around 10 months, I was finally diagnosed with Q-Fever
(a disease caused by infection with Coxiella burnetii which
affects both humans and animals). Even now, several years
later, I am still unwell.

'I have the biggest fear of dying and don't like to be
by myself. Every day is a struggle, and it was a strain on
my wonderful husband Tim and our five children. Tim
was only 36 when I became ill and our children were just
ten, eight, seven, six and five... young to be around such a
sick mother.

'I believe strongly in my heart that one day I will get
better. I am always looking for support and after reading
your books I was encouraged to ask my guardian angel
for some support and help every day. It really helped me;
up until that point I had never given much thought as to
whether I believed in angels or not. But I have always felt
that there was "something" out there, even though I didn't
know what it might be.

'At the time I became ill I was doing a few days'
voluntary work at the local Salvation Army shop every
week while the kids were at school. I absolutely loved it.
The people I worked with were all wonderful and fun to
be around. I was so sad to have to give up my work. I was
becoming so ill that I was unable to stand up for very long;
I found walking hard, so in the end I had no choice but to
stop volunteering.

'I constantly had fevers and was always in pain, dizzy and shaking. My life slowed down to the minimum. Sometimes I slept for up to 22 hours a day. I was unable to drive, and it got that bad that I could no longer look after my family or even myself. My lovely husband, Tim, took over everything.

'The kids grew up very quickly and they all got stuck in and helped out by making school lunches, doing the dishes, hanging out washing, sweeping floors and anything my husband asked them. I was so proud of the way they all rallied round. Tim's boss gave him time off work to look after me, and a few very good friends would come and stay with me; I was too scared to be by myself because I had such a fear of dying. I spent hours and hours on the phone to my mother for support, and my wonderful mother-in-law came to stay and looked after me, helping out when Tim couldn't take time off work and when we had to move from our home because I was becoming allergic to everything around me. It was at this time that I realized how lucky I was to have so many wonderful people in my life. If there was any blessing it was that… so many people loved and cared for me.

'Just after I got sick I remember sitting in our lounge one day and Tim and the kids were going about their business getting tea, doing homework and just playing. Even though I was sitting in the room, a part of me felt that I was outside looking in at us all. It seems I'd had a sort of out-of-body experience. It was like I was hovering above the ground just watching. I could even see myself, just sitting in the lounge. It was so very strange, I just put it out of my mind.

'At this time I was spending most hours of the day sleeping. I dreamed a lot, and most of the dreams I don't remember very well. But this particular "dream" was different. I remember it all very well like it happened yesterday. I've had dreams of flying before, but this was different, it was real.

'Not long after my out-of-body experience I was sleeping one night and woke abruptly. I felt like I'd landed on the bed with a big thump. My heart was beating fast and I just sat there for a long while. The strange thing is that I recalled exactly what I'd been doing before landing on my bed. I'd been flying with my friend Jan, who'd passed over only about a year earlier. This might sound strange, but we were flying around a huge mountain that had collapsed. There were people trapped everywhere and we were saving everyone. But even though it was a disaster, the place was so beautiful: there were waterfalls, trees and caves.

'I remember her holding my hand as we flew over a huge mountain. I knew there had been a landslide in the area we were flying over, and we were saving all these people and taking them to safety. The mountain was dark but the people we helped were all wearing bright clothes. We were dropping them by some big green trees with pink flowers all over them. We were getting people from caves and big rocks and putting them under the trees.

'My friend Jan never left my side once, but all of a sudden she let me go and started flying away. I followed her; she was flying towards something bright, through some fog, then she stopped and told me that I couldn't go with her, that I had to go back. As I'm stubborn I still followed her, but she stopped again and this time told me very clearly, "NO!" She told me, "You have to go back," and then all of a sudden I felt myself falling. That's when I hit the bed so hard that I thought I must have woken my husband up! As I came to I realized I was sitting up in bed, very stunned. I did tell my doctor about it and was put on anti-depressants, which unfortunately made me a lot sicker.

'Jan was one of Tim's bosses at work before she died of cancer. We were good friends through work. I had such respect for her. She was a wonderful person and a good boss. She always made me feel special. When we talked about the kids she was very supportive and encouraging, and loved to share stories. We were always on the same wavelength. We loved to laugh and talk, and I missed that when she left us.

'I went to visit Jan a couple of days before she died. She was so ill and fragile, but she still had her sense of humour. She joked about having tried to lose weight for years and now, because of the cancer, she was a lot thinner. I felt very guilty that I was not well enough to go to her funeral. Maybe Jan came to let me know that she was OK and to tell me that it was not my turn to die. I know that she forgives me for not going to her funeral. Maybe she was showing me that I still need to be here.

'The bright foggy stuff that Jan went through in my dream experience I now realize was heaven. I believe Jan wouldn't let me go with her because I had to stay on Earth to look after my family. I want so much to be well and strong again. I still have so much I want to do in my life.

'I did tell Tim about my experience when it happened. He just listened without judgement, as he always does. Jan *has never come to me in my dreams again, and I would love her to. I would love to know if she wants me to share this with any of her family. I think maybe she is now her own son's guardian angel and she was just sent to help me when I needed her. I just don't know. Is she still my angel? I am still none the wiser.*

'I have talked to Tim about angels, too, and what he believes, and he said, yes… he does believe in them to a degree. He thinks there is a possibility that something is there. I still don't understand a lot of the things that happened to me, but I'll tell you one thing: I can't wait for it to happen again. I talk to my angels all the time. I thank them every day for keeping me on this Earth with my family and helping me to get well again.' – TAMMIE

Finally a beautiful story of a passing over to the other side.

Angel in Waiting

'My mum had been suffering for many years with immobility due to a misdiagnosed fractured hip, then over the years her health deteriorated to the point where she was diagnosed with cancer a couple of years ago. I always thought this is what would take her in the end, but she battled and battled and stayed around to watch my daughter (her granddaughter) grow up (we lived upstairs and Mum lived downstairs in the same property).

'As her health deteriorated she started to suffer with fluid in her legs, which eventually spread up her body

and began to put pressure on her heart and lungs. After
a fall, she was rushed into hospital (it was a Thursday, I
remember). When I went to see her the doctor informed me
that it was congestive heart failure and she could go at
any time.

'Needless to say, the next few days were a complete
and utter blur. My mum, God bless her soul, was so brave.
She knew her time was coming and requested to see her
estranged daughter (my sister) before she passed over so
that the two of them could have this final time together.
No contact had been made for quite a while, so obviously
my sister would have known that any call she got from me
would be "the one". On the Saturday after Mum saw my
sister, she then requested that the priest from her parish
attend to her. She knew her time was coming and was
preparing for the last rites. She also requested to see my
daughter. Sunday was an extremely emotional day for the
family, and for Mum. With that she told my sister to return
home and that all she could take were visits from me.

'On Monday she took a turn for the worse; she began
to chatter to me in Polish (her native tongue) but I didn't
understand as I don't speak the language. She then began
to talk about things that had happened many months and
years before as if they were only yesterday, and I felt that
she was often elsewhere for much of the day. I knew her
time was close.

'On Tuesday I was told in the morning she was "stable"
when I called the hospital, then only half an hour later I got
"the call" to attend to Mum as her breathing had become
very laboured.

'When I got to the hospital I knew her final moments had finally arrived. I sat with her, spoke to her and held her hand. For a while I didn't think she knew I was there. I was sat at her right-hand side, and all of a sudden the air around her cooled. She turned her head to the left, opened her eyes and tried to speak. I could make out the words "No, not yet!"

'Someone had come for her. But as she said that she turned to me and told me she loved me and squeezed my hand so hard it was as if all her youthful strength had returned. Whoever had come for her seemed to stay for a while; I could tell as she kept turning her head towards them and I could feel a sense of peace in the room.

'At 1:05 p.m. my mum took her final breaths. I was so glad I was with her so she wasn't alone, and I was so glad someone was there to greet her and take her over to the other side. It also gave me a sense of peace, and something I will never forget: that when our time comes, we are not alone.

'This was only last week but I feel the presence of angels around me when I feel like I can't carry on. They give me the strength and love I need to get through this. Knowing my mum is being looked after on her new journey fills me with such happiness.' – Jola

Angels are real… the afterlife is real. There are so many recorded experiences of angels and afterlife experience, we've reached 'critical mass' – a time and a place where it's obvious that life goes on, and that while we are on the Earth we are protected and looked after by heavenly beings. Of course it's true!

I've really enjoyed sharing these magical and miraculous experiences with you. Naturally I have selected some of the more dramatic experiences for you to read, but even the simple and subtle experiences we encounter are valid. If you ask for help, watch out for an angel feather sign. Maybe your loved ones will visit you in a dream-type visitation experience. Don't forget what I've suggested here, and find yourself a lovely old photo of the deceased (if possible) or recall a special moment together to help make a connection with your loved one in heaven. Then you can begin to talk. You'll know that heavenly 'phone call' has been connected once you notice the emotion you have surrounding their loss – you'll feel a shift of sorts and may notice tears prick your eyes, or you may smile in remembrance of a special moment together. Simply ask for them to reach out to you in any way that they can. Dream visitation experiences are only one way – although it's my personal favourite!

Angels look after our loved ones, both human and animal; they take care of those dear to us, whether they are on the earthly or heavenly side of life. I think it's quite clear that angels are a real phenomenon and they are reaching out to humans more and more. So many people are having angel encounters; if you haven't had yours yet, don't worry – it's just a matter of time, so be patient.

Angel experiences, and mainly contact with deceased loved ones, have always been a part of my family. My sisters and I in particular have regular contact with our late uncle and father. Dad is as much a part of our lives these days as he was before he passed. You, too, can experience afterlife contact... simply ask for that sign!

Maybe, like me, you'll get sneaky tricks like snooker balls clacking together in the middle of the night (maybe it was Dad at that B&B – he was a keen snooker player!), or a member of your deceased family will start messing around with your computer files! Fishing indeed! Thanks for that one, Dad!

Remember they also flicker lights, play music, drop photographs, books and magazines in front of you, show you number plates and posters or mess around with your electrical and clockwork items. You'll never know what to expect, but it will always be wonderful. Don't let fear get in the way of a fantastic experience. Fear is the one emotion that stops the angel and afterlife contact. Remember, they are trying to lift our spirits, not scare us half to death!

I'm sad we've come to the end of another book, but if you feel you need more, then do explore the many wonderful sources of information and collections of these kinds of encounters out there (more about this in the list of Resources that follows).

Resources

Also by Jacky Newcomb:

Books

An Angel Held My Hand (HarperElement)

Angel Kids (Hay House)

An Angel by My Side (HarperElement)

An Angel Saved My Life (HarperElement)

Angel Secrets (Octopus)

An Angel Treasury (HarperElement)

Angels Watching Over Me (Hay House)

Call Me When You Get to Heaven (with Madeline Richardson; Piatkus)

Dear Angel Lady (Hay House)

A Faerie Treasury (with Alicen Geddes-Ward; Hay House)

Healed by an Angel (Hay House)

I Can See Angels (Hay House)

A Little Angel Love (HarperElement)

Angel Blessings (Octopus)

DVDs

Angels (New World Music)

CDs

Angel Cards on CD-Rom (Paradise Music)

Angel Workshop (workshop with meditations; Paradise Music)

Crystal Angels (instrumental by Llewellyn, cover notes by Jacky; Paradise Music)

Ghosthunting Workshop (with Barrie John; Paradise Music)

Healing with Your Guardian Angel (guided meditations; Paradise Music)

Meet Your Guardian Angel (guided meditations; Paradise Music)

Cards

Angel Secrets Cards (Octopus)

ABOUT THE AUTHOR

 **Jacky Newcomb** is a multi-award winning, *Sunday Times* bestselling author. She is the regular angel columnist for *Take a Break's Fate & Fortune* magazine. Jacky has published hundreds of articles about paranormal phenomena for magazines and e-zines all over the world. She is regularly featured in the UK national press and interviewed on radio and television, including ITV's *This Morning* and Channel 5's *LIVE with...*

Jacky gives talks and runs workshops all over the country, and talks to thousands of people each year. She's worked with many celebrity names – many of whom have become friends as well as fans of her work! Jacky is the expert the experts turn to!

'...successful author and broadcaster...' – *The Weekly News*

'I love Jacky's books!' – TV presenter Melissa Porter

'...Jacky Newcomb's books have made her a well-respected name in the study of angels and afterlife communication. Jacky's work is essential reading for anyone interested in learning more about this fascinating subject...' – Uri Geller

Jacky has an extensive website where you'll find free information and links to her Twitter site and Facebook page.

www.jackynewcomb.com

JOIN THE HAY HOUSE FAMILY

As the leading self-help, mind, body and spirit publisher in the UK, we'd like to welcome you to our family so that you can enjoy all the benefits our website has to offer.

 EXTRACTS from a selection of your favourite author titles

 COMPETITIONS, PRIZES & SPECIAL OFFERS Win extracts, money off, downloads and so much more

 LISTEN to a range of radio interviews and our latest audio publications

 CELEBRATE YOUR BIRTHDAY An inspiring gift will be sent your way

 LATEST NEWS Keep up with the latest news from and about our authors

 ATTEND OUR AUTHOR EVENTS Be the first to hear about our author events

iPHONE APPS Download your favourite app for your iPhone

 HAY HOUSE INFORMATION Ask us anything, all enquiries answered

join us online at **www.hayhouse.co.uk**

 292B Kensal Road, London W10 5BE
T: 020 8962 1230 E: info@hayhouse.co.uk